Fish Farming : For Pleasure & Profit.

THE

History of
Howietoun

CONTAINING A

Full Description

OF THE VARIOUS

HATCHING-HOUSES and PONDS, and of the EXP·· ··NTS

UNDERTAKEN from 1873 to 1886,

AND ALSO OF

THE FISH CULTURAL WORK

AND THE

MAGNIFICENT RESULTS OBTAINED.

By THE LATE

Sir J. RAMSAY=GIBSON=MAITLAND, Bart.,

F.L.S., F.G.S., F.Z.S., &c., &c.

Practical Advice on

Fish-Culture Matters

IS OFFERED BY THE AUTHOR OF

"Fish Farming: for Pleasure and Profit."

The Author of *Fish Farming: for Pleasure and Profit* is prepared to visit any part of the United Kingdom with the object of advising as to the formation of new fisheries, or the improvement of old ones. Estate waters surveyed; plans and working drawings prepared; every description of approved apparatus made and fixed; leaving all in perfect working order. Inquiries should be addressed to Mill House, Bradwell-on-Sea, Essex.

TO

Arthur Charles Bonsall,

In grateful recognition of much kindly encouragement received from him during the production of the book, by

THE AUTHOR.

CONTENTS.

—◆—

THE
Weston ❧
❧ Fishery,
NORWICH, ENGLAND,

Still maintains the reputation of being
one of the best fisheries in England
where

TROUT ARE REARED -
— ON —
- - A LARGE SCALE.

For over Thirty Years
A Steady Level of Excellence
Has been Maintained.

BROWN & RAINBOW TROUT SPECIALITIES.

COLONEL F. H. CUSTANCE, C.B. : : Proprietor.

SEND FOR PRICE LIST.

PREFACE.

ONE result of the publication of this work, I venture to hope, will be an increased interest in the simple improvement of existing fisheries and the formation of some new ones. But the result I should especially like to see is a proper application of the possibilities of fish-farming on sound business-like lines. I would like to see fish-culture become part and parcel of the education of those who rent or own the rivers, streams, lakes, and ponds of the British Isles; and I firmly believe that it will become so in the very near future. Then this volume, I trust, will be one—one of many; but always one—included in the fish-culturist's library. I am glad to say that this little work on " Fish Farming " goes to press with the most practical support and hearty good-will of almost all the fish-culturists of the British Isles and of not a few abroad. My note-book and camera have been busy over many months at the various establishments I have visited, and at each of these I have received invaluable help at the hands of the different owners, and a free permit to extend my knowledge for the benefit of my readers. This kindness I have acknowledged in the text wherever possible, but I would like, in this place, to express my sincere thanks for it, and especially to those who have enabled me to contribute numerous special articles and many photographs to magazines and periodicals as well as to collect material for this book.

The SOWLEY FISHERY

LYMINGTON, HAMPSHIRE.

CHAS. BRAUN - - Pisciculturist.

BROWN TROUT *(Salmo Fario).*

RAINBOW TROUT *(Salmo Irideus).*

LOCH LEVEN TROUT *(Salmo Levenensis).*

Specially cultivated with
a view of PERMANENTLY
benefiting Waters in : :
which they are placed. :

❀ ❀ ❀

FRY, YEARLINGS, -
- - TWO=YEAR=OLDS.

❀ ❀ ❀

PRICE LISTS FREE.

The Fishery may be inspected by appointment.

FISH FARMING:

FOR

PLEASURE AND PROFIT

BY "PRACTICAL."

" Fish culture promises to be eventually the origin or increase of revenue to private individuals, a source of national wealth, and certainly a great boon to the public in general."—FRANK BUCKLAND.

Fully Illustrated from Photographs and Drawings by the Author.

London:

PRINTED AND PUBLISHED BY THE BURLINGTON PUBLISHING COMPANY, LIMITED
72, 73, 74, 75, AND 76 TEMPLE CHAMBERS, E.C.

1903.

FISH FARMING:

FOR

PLEASURE AND PROFIT.

CHAPTER I.

INTRODUCTORY.

Throughout a long and closely applied experience of fishing and fish-culture in the British Isles I have repeatedly been impressed by the enormous importance of the results awaiting the practical cultivation in this country of many hundreds of miles of stream and river and thousands of acres of lakes that at present lie waste; and I have again and again marvelled at the utterly neglected possibilities that present themselves in almost endless variety and on almost every side for the formation of fisheries. There are very few existing fisheries that could not be considerably improved, more especially in the direction of the proper protection of natural redds ---i.e., spawning grounds---or the construction and protection of artificial redds; and there are streams and brooks on nearly every estate that at little expense, by the simple construction of a dam here and there, and the erection of a few sluices and screens, could be transformed into capital trout ponds, if not, indeed, valuable sporting lakes. As a matter of fact, nearly every tiny brooklet that does not entirely dry up during summertime is sufficient to supply the necessary water for one or more fish ponds, the exceptions to this rule being very few indeed and very far between. Yet year after year, generation after generation, farmers and landowners daily pass these "insignificant" brooks, and do not realise the great value of the possibilities that lie to their hand, not only from a sporting point of view, but in a pecuniary sense also. Acre for acre, cultivated water pays much better than cultivated land, and the

AN ARTIFICIAL TROUT LAKE.

expense of such cultivation is not more—often less. Then, again, consider the large sums of money spent every year by anglers in visiting distant fisheries, principally because good sport with trout or other fish does not exist in their own immediate neighbourhood. Yet probably a splendid sporting water could be formed actually on land the sportsman himself occupies at the cost of two or three such angling expeditions. True, one does not always want to fish at one's own back door, but it is passing strange that more good fishing does not exist at the back doors of more anglers. And it must not be forgotten that, as I have said, the fisheries generally—where they do exist—are not cultivated as they should be. Hence, turn where wo may, sport is not what it could and should be.

This state of affairs cries aloud for amendment. If there were no demand for the sporting rights of waters containing Salmonidæ, and if salmon and trout were not valuable additions to the Nation's food supply, I could understand, although I could not appreciate, this neglect. But, seeing that large rentals accrue to the proprietors of salmon and trout waters for sporting purposes, that the fish command a high price in the food market, that in both instances the demand greatly exceeds the supply, and that, consequently, waters containing Salmonidæ are a valuable asset to any and every estate, and to the Nation at large, one is quite at a loss to understand the apathy that exists.

Perhaps I should rather have said did exist; for at the present time there are indications of some interest being taken in fish-culture and the formation of fisheries in this country. Genuine enthusiasm is wanting among us, but something better than mere spasmodic efforts is in evidence; and one is encouraged to believe that the present wave of interest in pisci-culture is likely to gather force. The formation and cultivation of sporting waters lies to the hand of the estate owners and their tenants; the future of this valuable National asset rests really with them, and to this fact some proprietors would appear to be wakening up. All of them are not anglers, but all have friends who are, and from their own or from other's experience they are realising the value of sporting waters. They are discovering also that the requisite management need not entail heavy outlay. When this is recognised, so also is the folly of having miles of water flow barren to the sea, which at comparatively small cost might teem with fish, or of allowing a sporting water to be depleted because of the failure to expend upon it a few pounds annually.

Many proprietors within the last few years have made a start with practical experiments; many more are on the eve of doing so. But the problems of fish-culture are many, and

to the uninitiated, often difficult.   In every piece of water to
be dealt with there are natural conditions calling for some
modifications of the normal operations of fish-culture.   No
doubt, the several owners will quickly learn by experience.
They will learn from their failures.   These initial failures,
however, are apt in many cases to damp enthusiasm, and in
any case they waste valuable time, probably when the critical
condition of the water makes expedition urgent.   Therefore,

THE SAME, SHOWING POSITION OF SPAWNING GROUNDS.

with a view to assist owners in their efforts, I place before them
information culled from many quarters, in as simple and as
practical a manner as I can, feeling sure that some benefit, at
least, must result.

I am prepared for the objection, " Successful cultivation of
sporting waters necessitates long years of study and practice,"
and willingly admit that at certain stages fish-culture requires
the exercise of considerable scientific and practical knowledge
in combination if the best results are to be obtained.   But the
delicate processes of spawning fish, incubating eggs in the

early stages, and feeding the very young fry, which go to " fill
the bill " of objection to the carrying out of such advice as I
tender in the following pages, are not necessarily included in
the formation of and profitable cultivation of sporting waters,
although they are such a fascinating study that the operator
will inevitably include them in his programme later on. Such
operations, however, may be left in the hands of the expert at
present, and the owner of any water may pick up the thread
of cultivation where the expert's assistance is required in a
lesser degree.

Granted, however, that practical knowledge is as valuable
in the cultivation of water as it is in the farming of land,
surely when such a rich harvest awaits those who choose to
farm the waters sufficient practical knowledge of fish-culture
becomes as necessary to complete the education of those who
farm or own estates as the knowledge of how to grow hops,
wheat, and turnips, and how to raise fat stock and poultry.
For this reason in their proper place I have given instructions
in these more delicate processes.

Personally, I am inclined to think that to gather the rich
harvest our waters offer means only—or, at any rate, in a
very large measure—application. Further, I am convinced
that, even if a whole generation of close application be necessary to the practical requirements associated with the successful stocking of our waters with Salmonidæ, and the making
and stocking of others, it would be time well spent, for the reward would, indeed, be most handsome. But there is no reason, to my mind, why those who sow should not reap also in
the near future. In the following pages I have laid down
the methods by which sporting waters may be formed and the
most modern principles of pisciculture may be simply and successfully applied to their practical cultivation. The advice
given, whether it refers to the construction of apparatus, the
formation and management of fish-ponds, the rearing of fish,
or any other of the numerous matters dealt with, may be absolutely relied upon as being the outcome of the joint experi-
ences of the leading pisciculturists throughout the world,

coupled with the honest observations of one who has no axe to grind, no fish to sell. To a large extent, the measure of success attained by those who practically test the value of the

THE REDDS TO THE LAKE.

advice will depend upon the exercise of some common-sense on their own part. They may, however, start with the firm conviction, after perusing these pages, that the way has been made smoother for them than was the case with their immediate predecessors. Every structure and all the apparatus illustrated are

in actual existence, and answer their purpose admirably; but
I do not deny that the present-day methods of cultivating Salmonidæ, excellent as they undoubtedly are, remain open to
further improvement, and such improvement may occur even
as I write.

I would encourage my readers from the first, and with this
object my first photographs are of an artificially-formed trout
lake, situated at the Earl of Denbigh's Welsh home at Holywell,
North Wales. It is a splendid sporting water, and is self-supporting, i.e., there are spawning grounds in connection with it,
so that the fish may in season run up from the lake to the redds
in quite a natural manner. Yet where this lake now is once

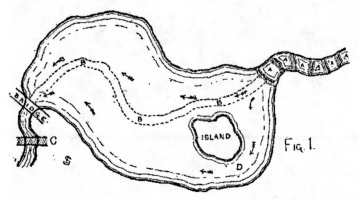

Fig. 1.

ran an insignificant brooklet that held only tiny troutlings.
After a simple manner the water has been dammed back to
form the lake and the redds have been made by forming a
succession of small pools and falls. The tiny troutlings no
longer exist, but in their place are some very fine brown
trout, S. Fario, which provide excellent sport for the proprietor and his friends. It is not too much to say that there are
hundreds of similar brooklets in this country that could
be treated in a like successful manner. If only I can show
" how it is done," my object will be obtained.

Fig. 1 is an imaginary plan of such a lake as that illustrated.
The shape of the banks render it only necessary to dam back
the water at a most convenient spot c, and, Presto! the work
is half accomplished. It becomes necessary also, however, to

form the island, or otherwise the debris from up stream will inevitably gradually silt up in the bend at D. Next, the redds are formed at A A A A A A.   The dotted lines B B B show the original bed of the brook.   The arrows show the direction of the current.   The dam is built at C, instead of, as might well be supposed, at the point where the bridge is, because the bank on the right hand is very high, and forms a natural support to the heavy volume of water contained in the lake.

The formation of a fishing pool or the cultivation of an existing fishery is not always a simple matter; but the very worst obstacles are not insurmountable—if you only go about it in the right way.   That is what I want to try and do— to put you in the right way.

CHAPTER II.

NATURAL AND ARTIFICIAL REDDS.

Before dealing in detail with the construction of ponds and lakes, I propose to say something about redds. By "redds"

NATURAL SPAWNING GROUNDS.

is meant those parts of a stream where fish (for our present purpose, trout) spawn. The redds in connection with the artificial trout lake that I have illustrated as an example of what can be done by the formation of a fishery, where previously only a brook existed, have been artificially formed also, and are really an after-part of the work of making a fishing pool that shall be self-supporting.

The reason why I deal with them and with natural and artificial redds generally in this place is because the protection of natural redds and the formation of protected artificial redds are by far the most simple and inexpensive methods of improving existing fisheries; indeed, in many cases they are, or one or the other is, the only thing necessary to be done—so long as it is done thoroughly. Yet how often it remains undone! Take, for instance, the river Teign, South Devenshire, which is the subject of the next three illustrations. I have purposely pho-

NATURAL SPAWNING GROUNDS.

tographed those parts of the river where magnificent redds exist; and, properly handled, these should thoroughly stock the whole of the river of which they form such picturesque parts. Yet, as a matter of fact, that same river is, comparatively speaking, fishless. Let us see how this deplorable state of affairs could be remedied.

When the spawning season arrives, i.e., about the end of October, trout mount up from the deeper and heavier waters to the feeders of the lake, or to the upper parts of, or the tributaries to, the stream that may be their home. Seeking shallow water, and, if possible, a clean, gravelly bottom, where the current is fairly sharp but does not rush or tear along, the female fish deposits her eggs, the male fish sheds his milt over them, and thereafter they are left to the anything but tender mercies of their numerous enemies, and the destructive forces of floods and other unfavourable circumstances. The result is that on unprotected redds only a very, very small percentage of eggs are hatched. Now, it should be noticed that the photographs are, as I have said, of magnificent spawning grounds, but they are unprotected; hence the failure of them for productive purposes. Of remedies there are several.

Where apparatus and facilities exist for the purposes of artificially incubating and hatching the eggs, the ripe fish may be caught from the redds and spawned, as will hereafter be described. For the present I presume such facilities to be nonexistent; therefore, to obtain satisfactory results without them the redds must be handled in a practical manner. And, in passing, I should add that where no redds exist they should be formed. This is a simple matter, and the photograph of the redds to the lake shows a most serviceable and easily arranged succession of spawning grounds, made by converting a noisy, rushing brooklet into a " step by step " series of sober, glassy glides and miniature falls. Natural spawning grounds similar to those illustrated are quite easily arranged as splendid redds under complete control, the work consisting principally in shifting and arranging the boulders in the bed of the stream so as to get a series of small " flats " and shallow falls, rather than one or two pools, which may be capital natural spawning grounds, but are not the best arrangement for the purpose of protected redds. It is important that redds should be get-at-able from either bank. They should range from twenty to not more than, say, fifty feet in length. The width is governed by circumstances. They should be from four inches to eight inches in depth, but a foot is not too much. They should be well and finely gravelled, and a full and evenly distributed current of water should flow over them. This ar-

rangement is not difficult to arrive at, and is best manipulated
at the falls. The nearer the redds approach this pitch of perfection the better.

Before the fish mount to spawn it should be ascertained that
the redds are free from enemies to fish eggs—including fish !—
and an arrangement of screens should be at hand to place across
the stream. The making of and the method of fixing these

NATURAL SPAWNING GROUNDS.

screens is fully dealt with in the chapter on that subject. As
soon as the fish are on the redds a watchful eye becomes necessary, and at this stage it is as well that you should be made
acquainted with two important facts. First, that the early
spawners are the fish to be made use of; and, secondly, that
the best eggs are obtained from well-matured parents. Hence,
it follows that young trout should not be allowed to remain on
protected redds; send them about their business; net
them out, or drive them away to attend to their domestic
affairs elsewhere. But as soon as the early, well-matured
spawners are on the redds in sufficient numbers, put the
screens in position and let them spawn in peace. As soon as

possible after they have spawned they should be netted out
and replaced in the water whence they came. This can easily
be done if the redds are properly formed or wisely chosen, and,
as I have said, easily get-at-able from either bank. In most
cases the fish will drop down stream and be found in the lower
water right against the screen, and the job is then simplified;
often enough, indeed, one need only lift the screen and the fish
will, of their own accord, bolt into the lake or river. Under
these latter circumstances be careful to replace the screen at
once, and make sure that no other fish run up to the redds.
From the time that a sufficiency of eggs has been spawned
until the fry are allowed to escape at will—a matter dealt with
in the chapter on stocking—the screens must be kept in
position; the principal reason for this being the necessity of
keeping other fish from intruding on the redds, for if they are
allowed to do so they will assuredly root among the good
eggs, probably eat them, or, at least, do something objectionable. Their idea is to spawn themselves, and, as they are
later, and probably in other ways less desirable fish, you do not
want them. Moreover, often enough these late fish visit the
redds with the one and only object of eating the eggs. Later
on, the alevins and fry would suffer in a similar manner from
the same cause.

The two next matters that concern us are the answers to
two questions that most probably have occurred to your mind:
When is a trout well matured? and what constitutes a sufficiency of eggs? Well, an ordinary British brown trout arrives
at maturity in its third year, but the best eggs are obtained
from it in the fourth, fifth, and sixth years. The size of the
fish varies considerably in different waters, but, speaking
generally, it is not worth while to protect the eggs of fish of
less than one pound in weight, and a pound and a half or a
two-pounder fish is to be preferred. After the seventh year the
eggs deteriorate in value, and it may be generally relied on
that very old spawners—you will soon learn to tell them—are
as useless as very young fish. You must have some knowledge of
the fish in the particular water you are interested in before

you can for certainty recognise a suitable spawner on the redds, and until you gain that knowledge err on the right side, and only protect the eggs of trout not less than one pound. In these matters common sense must guide you. Mayhap there is not a pounder in the water, and a fish of half that weight is well worthy of reception on your protected redds. As a rule, the early spawners are the heavier fish in any water, so that your early spawners are probably a fair sample of the available stock for reproductive purposes. Nevertheless, a good brace or two may turn up late, and I must leave their case to your own discretion. At any rate, include the best fish available in your operations, if at all possible, and do not forget that the eggs from two or three brace of well-matured fish are of far more value for your purpose than those of quadruple the number from doubtful fish. Remember also that your four-year-old fish may be a two-pounder; if so, all the better, as long as it has attained that weight in a natural manner, i.e., that it is not a fish that has been artificially forced with horse-flesh only on a commercial fish-farm.

Sufficiency of eggs. This, of course, absolutely depends upon the extent of the fishery to be stocked and the size of the redds. A golden rule is to limit the number to the absolute requirements of the case; rather have too few than too many. Your success depends not upon the thousands of eggs spawned so much as upon the room you have on the redds for the alevins (as the young fish are called when first hatched) and the feed in the water for the fry (as the young fish are called when they start to feed, and on to the yearling stage). This latter is a most important matter, and I deal with it at length later on. The best advice I can give you is to have too few eggs the first year of your operations. Afterwards you will better know what your redds can carry with profit. To start with, a redd thirty to fifty feet long and from one to three yards wide should have to provide for not more than three to six well-matured spawners; and, in your early operations, at least, it is inadvisable to allow more on a redd of that size. An average four-year-old fish should carry 1,000 eggs, so

that on your redd you have somewhere about three to six
thousand eggs. Of course, with very fine spawners the number will be considerably more, and even fewer fish will suffice.
Later on, when you are better acquainted with the working of
the redds, they may be permitted to carry fair more eggs.

So far, it will be gathered, we have merely formed artificial
redds or utilised natural ones, and simply protected them by
placing screens at the ends of the series. And, where circumstances are favourable, this is all that is necessary. It will be
noticed that I am dealing only with those redds under control;
other natural redds there may be close at hand even, or somewhere on the estate. These need not concern you; they may
be left to take their chance if the protected redds are sufficient
for your purpose. But they may receive a little outside help
at your hands, with benefit both to them and you. As a matter of fact, the protected redds should be sufficient for the purpose of stocking your waters. But they may need other protection than that of the screens. For instance, floods may
come, and these most certainly demand precaution. Then,
again, the redds we have had under consideration are formed
or exist directly on the stream. It is quite possible that you
may have a good fishing river, but not a length of it suitable
for redds on your estate; therefore, they must be made off the
main stream. In this connection I may at once state that
redds formed off a stream are for many reasons better than
those formed direct on one; but they are a little more trouble
to make, and are slightly more expensive, although a decent
carpenter and a labourer or two for a few days constitute the
principal outlay.

Fig. 2 at once makes clear the method of protecting a series
of redds from flood, etc., when they are formed direct on a
stream. A A A A are the redds; B B B B are falls; C C are
screens (notice that the screens are placed at an acute and
obtuse angle across the water and not at right angles to either
bank; the reason for this is explained in the chapter on
"Screens"); D D, D are the sluices; E is the outlet for the
surplus water, at which point a simple contrivance for pre-

venting fish mounting up surplus-water channels, and other places where they are not wanted, is fixed. I give a photograph

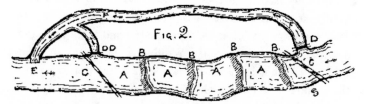

Fig. 2.—Method of Protecting Redds against Flood, etc.

of this contrivance, which I think explains itself. It is in use at the Earl of Denbigh's fishery at Bronedd, North Wales. All

CONTRIVANCE FOR PREVENTING FISH RUNNING UP SURPLUS
WATER CHANNELS, ETC.

I need say concerning it is that it is at once the most simple, economical, and effective arrangement of its sort that I have met with. In fixing take care that the whole body of water strikes against the slanting front board, which should extend below the point where the water strikes it. Should the water flow out at E, on a level with the main stream, a screen should be used in place of the contrivance; but so arrange it, if possible, that a fall occurs at this point, for there is nothing to be gained by having to put a screen there, and it is a rule without exception to have as few screens as possible in any fishery, as, even under most favourable conditions of fixing and situation, they invariably require some attention, and the saving of labour is a consideration at every fishery; F F F is the surplus water channel, which be sure to have cut deep enough. The sluice at D D is for the purpose of disposing of any debris that may accumulate against the screen c. All these matters will be explained fully in their proper place.

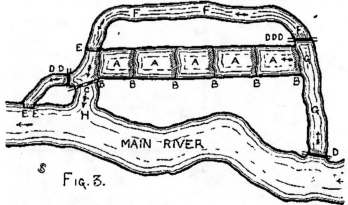

Fig. 3.—Method of Constructing Redds off a River.

The direction of the current is shown by the arrows. The working of the arrangement is quite simple. The use of the screens I have already explained (and they will be referred to again when I am dealing with rearing the young fish). The sluice at D is adjusted so that sufficient, and only sufficient, water passes over the redds, the surplus being conducted down the channel F F F and so out into the main stream at E. In this manner the redds are guarded against any but a most disastrous flood, and they should not be formed at all where such a flood is likely to occur. Of course, the outlet E may occur at any point lower down, as most convenient; indeed, it should be lower down than shown; and equally, of course, the series of redds may be longer or shorter, and, indeed, there

C

may be two or more series; but in such case each series should
be screened off and a sluice fixed as D D at C.

Fig. 3 requires a little more explanation. It will, however,
be seen that by this arrangement the redds are under absolutely complete control. But even in this case I strongly advise you to choose a position where there occurs least risk of a
big flood.

It often happens, though, that such a position is not
attainable on an estate; and, if this be so, an arrangement of
redds formed off a river such as here shown should be—with
care and attention at the critical time—quite free from
any unfortunate results. A A A A A are the redds; B B B B B B
the falls; C is the only screen required; D D D, D D, D are
sluices; E E is the outlet for debris and surplus water from
sluice D D; E is the main outlet from the surplus water channel F F F; at E E a contrivance for preventing fish running up
may advisedly be placed; at E one must be put, or a screen
may be put in place of a contrivance, but the latter is much
to be preferred, for reasons already stated; F F F is the
surplus water channel; G G is the supply channel to the
redds; H is the main outlet from the redds. In the spawning
season the fish will run up at H; the screen C is then put into
position; the fish are prevented from running up the channel
at E, therefore they mount to the redds. If the fall at the
top end of the redds, at G, cannot be made of sufficient height
to prevent fish mounting up it, another arrangement of
the supply channel becomes advisable, and this is
shown in Fig. 4 and Fig. 5; otherwise the fish will
mount into the channel G G. This latter arrangement is also
advisedly adopted where the sluice D is not absolutely proof
against fish dropping down stream and over it; indeed, I
should always advise its adoption, only that where possible
the aeration occurring from a decent fall at G, at the head of
the redds, is most beneficial.

Fig. 4 is a plan of an underground supply to the redds, and
Fig. 5 is a section of same through N O. Here again A is the
top redd, the width of which from P to R is purposely shortened

in the drawing to prevent it taking up too much space; G is
the supply channel; F is the surplus water channel; D D D
the sluice. All these references are purposely identical with
those of Fig. 3. In this case the water, instead of falling
direct from G into A, is separated therefrom by a solid earth

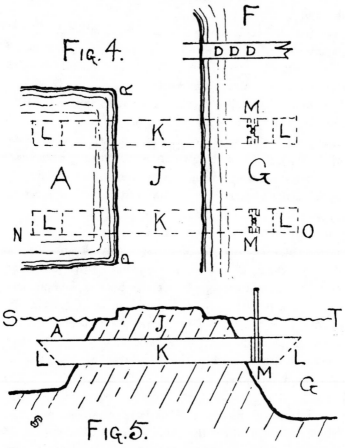

Figs. 4 and 5.—Plan and Section of Underground Water Supply.

bank J, and the water is really conducted underground
through square wooden channels, made after the manner of
very elongated boxes. Two or more of these channels may
be used according to the size of the redds. Have a sufficiency
of them by all means; they are easily enough made and fitted.
A convenient size for them is six inches square, inside mea-

surement. The ends of the channels are covered by slanting perforated zinc screens. They are slanted, and in the manner shown, to get the greatest available surface and to prevent, as far as possible, debris accumulating on them. These screens may be made to slide in and out, but it is not necessary nor advisable, as they are apt to be left out. The supply of water through the channels is controlled by a small hand sluice at M, which in the drawing is shown shut down. The line s T is the highest level to which the water in either the redd A or the channel G should be permitted to rise. This level can always be adjusted at the sluices D D D and D (in Fig. 3). Do not attempt to adjust the height of water in the channel G by means of the hand sluices M; they are merely to regulate the supply to the redds. Six inches of water at least is maintained in the channel G above the top of the wooden channels. These wooden channels ought never to block, but should anything of that nature occur, off with the screens at each end, lift the hand sluice right out, and, if necessary (which can hardly ever be the case) force the obstacle out from either end. The channels are shown parallel to the surface, but they may be made to fall—from G to A, never from A to G. With a normal supply of water in the main river, only a small quantity need be flowing over the sluice D D D; but in case of flood adjust all three sluices (in Fig. 3), so that as much water as possible passes through the surplus water channel and out at H and E E (also Fig. 3). Do not forget, however, that no obstruction exists in the main river, which should be the principal means of disposing of flood water in the ordinary way. In the drawing the shape of the redds, the surplus water channel, and the main river are, of course, merely supposed; the real shape depends upon the contour of the banks, but the redds should be formed in as direct line as possible, in order to ensure an even flow of water over them.

I do not recommend the formation of protected redds in positions that present great natural difficulties. It may happen, however, that the only spawning grounds on one's own estate are so situated, and then it becomes necessary to

protect the eggs from being swept away by the first flood—
and floods pretty generally occur during the season of incubation—or otherwise destroyed. In Fig. 6 I suppose a stream
in the hills is confined between high banks; that the levels of
the surrounding countryside do not permit of a channel being
cut, as shown in connection with my remarks on how to construct ponds in hilly districts in the chapter on that subject,
and that consequently the redds must be protected absolutely
in the bed of the river itself.

Choose a favourable spot, if possible where the current will
naturally be inclined to flow towards the channel c c, and
form a substantial breakwater D B B, which must be sufficiently
high to protect the redds from any possible flood. Above the
dotted line D the bed of the stream, and consequent depth of
water, must be arranged so as to ensure a constant supply of
water flowing through the "underground" supply channels
E E E (which are made and fixed as explained in Fig. 4 and
Fig. 5), when the water is at its lowest level. Below the
dotted line D the channel c c must be well deepened, and the
adjoining bank may, if possible, be encroached upon; the
material so obtained being used in the construction of the
breakwater. These precautions become necessary in order to
facilitate the passage of a great push of water through the
channel c c. It will be noticed that the screen F is, of necessity in this case, cleared from debris by a sluice at the end
nearest the bank, and not by a channel cut into the bank, as
in Fig. 2 and Fig. 3. The redds are marked at A. The falls
to them should be arranged to permit of extra deep falls at
J and K, especially at J; this to guard against the flood water
flowing back on the lower redds. If possible, the fall of the
river from the point G to the point H should exceed the probable rise of water at flood time; if this is so, then you need
fear nothing from flood water flowing back over the redds,
but if it be less then you are sure to get some sediment on the
eggs after the flood subsides. This is certainly not in your
favour; but it can be dealt with, if it does not occur in too ex-
aggerated a form, in the manner explained at the end of this

chapter. In arranging the depth of the falls at J and H—and, for that matter, any other falls in any other position in any other fishery—you must be acquainted with the fact that a fish cannot surmount them, and consequently cannot mount upstream, unless the depth of water at the foot of the fall is equal to the height of the fall. This rule is not without exception, but it may be applied generally, and especially in connection with the construction of redds. If the stream is subject to such heavy floods as would undoubtedly result in the redds being covered entirely with flood water flowing back against the less strong current emanating from the channels E E E, then abandon any thought of constructing protected redds in

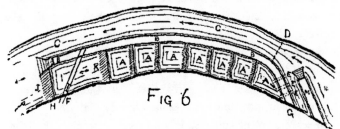

Fig. 6.—Method of Protecting Redds in Bed of River.

that position. Similar advice applies to the breakwater M; under normal conditions it is not required at all, but should the flood be sufficiently strong to bring down heavy debris it should be erected in order to protect the inlets of the channels E E E; and if the little valley holds a roaring torrent, sweeping all before it at flood time, then the breakwater (or any other contrivance) is useless, and the position is not suitable for constructing redds. At spawning time you will probably get your share of fish on the redds (of course, the screen F is not in position until you have a sufficient number of spawning fish on the redds), but, should they prefer the channel C C, you must place some obstruction to them mounting (preferably, a screen at the lower end of the channel), which must be removed at any sign of flood, or after spawning operations are over, and you care little whether fish mount the channel or not.

As a rule a stream presents some possibility for the formation of redds off it, as in Fig. 3, and, even if those redds have to be half a mile or more away from the bank of the main stream, it is preferable to their construction as in Fig. 6, which plan should only be adopted when compulsory.

In any case, do not let your redds be too large; rather have more occupying the same space. It is very useful to have light, galvanised wire-netting frames at hand to place across each redd and thus separate it from the others. The earliest fish mount up to the top redd and may be confined there; then the redd next below becomes the available spawning ground; and so on, until all the series are occupied. If any fish should spawn in the lower redds before the upper redds are occupied, then temporarily protect their eggs in the manner explained later on in this chapter. As soon as the fish have spawned on either redd they may be taken out. As soon as all the fish on the redds have spawned the light wire frames may be taken away altogether, but the main screens must remain in position for reasons already stated.

The scarcity of natural redds, and neglect in the formation of artificial redds in connection with many of our lakes and ponds, are the cause, in a very large measure, of the depleted state of those waters. I hope I have made clear the remedy. In most cases its application is a simple matter; but, of course, there exist conditions that absolutely bar the rendering of any assistance in the way of redds, and these must be dealt with by other methods of stocking, of which I have something to say later on.

Having made and protected the reeds you have done well, and your fishery is bound to profit from the little care and attention you have given it, for, without doubt, protected redds are far more prolific than those unprotected. There remain a few other useful hints to be imparted. The first of these is concerning shade. Fish eggs require shade, and plenty of it, and it is equally necessary to the well-being of the alevins and fry—and, indeed, for that matter, is more or less necessary throughout the whole conduct of a fishery. If

you take another glance at the photographs of natural spawning grounds, you will see that in each case the banks of the
river are well wooded. If this shade does not exist in connection with artificially formed redds, it must be provided,
either by planting trees or by placing covers over the redds.
I deal with the subject of enemies to fish eggs in another chapter; but I may say here that protection from birds is pretty
well sure to be necessary.   The best plan is to enclose the
redds entirely with either tanned netting or light galvanised wire netting; the top frame may, where necessary, serve
the purpose of a shade also. It will frequently happen that
one or two valuable fish will spawn before the bulk of fish are
on the redds, and it becomes necessary to protect these very
early eggs from being up-rooted by other later, yet sufficiently
desirable, spawners. This is best done by an arrangement of
wire-netting framed on galvanised iron frames (after the manner of very large pea-protectors), but care must be exercised
that the netting does not get clogged with debris, and so prevent a proper current of water from flowing over the eggs.
Ova may be, and advisedly is, protected in a similar manner
in the open in big waters, but it is, of course, far more easily
and effectually protected on properly controlled redds.

Should the fishery be short of mature spawners, or should
the introduction of new blood be deemed advisable, fully-
eyed ova may be sown on the redds; indeed, this is a most
valuable method of improving an existing fishery where there
are protected redds. The gravel should be raked level in a
suitable spot, and the eyed eggs sown very thinly over it, and
then left to hatch. In this way you will get a much larger
percentage hatched out than if the eggs were naturally
spawned, principally because the ova is delivered almost on
the point of hatching, and consequently has to run the gaunt-
let of its enemies for a few days only instead of for nearly three
months. This ova is also quite easily and very advantageously
handled in simple outside hatcheries, which will be described
in their proper place. Caution is necessary in connection with
the purchase of fully-eyed ova. Obtain the eggs from some tho

roughly responsible commercial fish-culturist, and be careful to get true strains of Fario only, until you are aquainted with the characteristics of other varieties of trout and are fully persuaded as to the advisability of introducing them into your fishery. You are pretty safe with Fario; you may not be with the others. Most certainly Levenensis and Irideus are both useful in their proper place, but wait until you have read what I have to say about them before sowing their eggs on your redds.*

The length of time occupied in the incubation of the eggs varies considerably, and is controlled principally by the temperature of the water. It may be eighty days, and it may be more than one hundred; but do not concern yourself about this, for often enough the longer the time in incubation the stronger the alevins. Do not disturb the eggs from the time they are spawned until they hatch, but should they become covered with sediment, which is plainly to be seen, let a stronger volume of water down over them for a few hours—but not sufficient to wash them from their bed. See that no debris accumulates to prevent an even and constant supply of water flowing over the eggs, and you will run but little risk from sediment. Two months after spawning a slightly greater volume of water may be permitted to flow over the eggs, and this may be increased very gradually until they begin to hatch. As soon as the greater bulk of eggs are hatched out, quite a respectable current of water may be sent over the alevins, and when the alevins have lost their umbilical sac (all of which matters will be presently explained), run plenty of water over the fry—as much, indeed, as is possible without washing up the gravel or driving the young fish against the screen below.

I have yet to tell you how best to supply the necessary food for the young fish. In this place I need only say that the screens, while being fine enough to keep predatory fish and some other objectionable characters off the redds, are coarse enough to permit the fry leaving the redds at will. And this

---

* See chapter on Rainbow, and Other Foreign Trout.

they do in large numbers.   From the end of June onward to
the next spawning season the screens may be taken up and
mature fish allowed free access to the redds.   Some are sure
to put in an appearance, and this will encourage them to the
proper position in which they are intended to help on your
operations for another year.   Just before spawning time run
plenty of water over the redds, and in other ways get them
into good order.   If no spate has occurred, you can easily
arrange for one after a simple manner, and this also should
be done.

I have emphasised the importance of being able to cope with
floods.   I would, in concluding my remarks on natural and
artificial redds, draw particular attention to the folly of
forming them where the stream is at all likely to dry up.
Such folly spells disaster.

CHAPTER III.

THE FORMATION OF PONDS AND LAKES.

Where ponds and lakes already exist they may, in most cases, be much improved in some way by following the instructions I now give for the formation of others, more especially in connection with the proper placing of screens and outlets, and the construction of surplus water channels. In some cases they can be brought under complete control—and if this is so so much the better. Mill-heads especially present excellent opportunities for the formation of spawning redds and rearing ponds for stocking purposes, close alongside, as there is sure to exist a good fall from the water above the mill to that below. Of course, the mill-heads I allude to are in connection with mills that do not send any poisonous refuse into the stream. If such millers generally would only recognise the favourable position they are in to construct a fishery that would most handsomely remunerate them for any trouble and expense they might be put to in connection with its formation and conduct, a very big thing would be done to restore our depleted waters, and a much better understanding would exist between millers and anglers.

And, while I am upon the subject, I would draw attention to the usefulness of protecting all rivers and streams in at least a portion of their length. The spasmodic efforts in connection with the so-called re-stocking of our waters—which in many cases merely means robbing Peter to pay Paul, and often enough spells the depletion of one water with no actual beneficial results to the other—are as ill-timed and as ill-judged as they are all insufficient. The proprietor of a water, or some association that rents the sporting rights of it, purchase from some commercial fish-farm, or obtain from some other water on the Peter v. Paul principle, a number of fish-eggs, fry, yearlings, or two-year-olds, and, casting them in, consider they have stocked their water. And so they may have done; but it is far more probable that they have done nothing of the sort. Most of the seed thus sown falls on barren ground. If it is proposed to sow fish-eggs I have shown how the ground must be prepared. If it is proposed to plant fish the ground

A PROTECTED, OR SCREENED, RIVER.

needs equally careful preparation. Consider what can be done by screening off a length of water, as shown in the next photograph, which is a view on the river at Mr. H. H. Gray's fishery at Hyde End, Brimpton, Berks., and therein rearing yearlings to the two-year-old stage; and surely I am not to be told that this is a difficult or costly operation! Yet yearlings are again and again placed haphazard in unprotected rivers and expected to produce good results, although want of food will polish one-third of them off and cannibalism account for yet another third of their number. Moreover, if we take Fig. 2 as a plan of such a protected length of stream, only substituting the plain river bed for the series of redds, the vast possibilities are at once evident. The surplus water can be made to supply redds formed off the river, as in Fig. 3, and, further, to provide the volume of water necessary for a set of rearing ponds. Thus, right under your hand you would have a complete fishery, from which each season might be obtained eggs, fry, yearlings—and two-year-olds ready for the rod or market. Under such circumstances you are really stocking your water, not " stocking-at it." Beyond doubt, if we are to replenish our depleted waters throughout the kingdom we must breed suitable fish under suitable conditions, not only at commercial fish-farms, but also in every other available position.

The most suitable ponds for farming fish are those that are made with that object, and one of the most simple forms of artificial ponds is shown in my next photograph, which is a view of the ponds at Eastgate, attached to Col. F. H. Custance's Weston Fishery, near Norwich. In this case a brook flows through some undulating meadow land, and, by a simple process, shown in Fig. 7, one or more trout pools are formed on it that may be used for sporting purposes only, or emptied at will, and the fish sold or used for stocking other waters. The drawing shows only one pond; but, of course, others can be formed on the same brook, after a similar manner, if only the fall or distance, or both, between them permits of the surface of water in the lower pond being below the level of the bottom of the pond next above it. If the fall does not permit of this, or if distance is not available and room has to be economised, and yet more than one pond is required, then a more complicated problem arises, and it is dealt with in Fig. 8.

Now, there are two very important conditions that go to make a really serviceable trout pond. These are, first, the convenient disposal of surplus or flood water; and, second, means of controlling the height of water in the pond and emptying it at will. In a series of ponds it becomes necessary also that each pond can be controlled independent of the others, and that any number of them in any position, or all of them together, can be handled after a similar manner. Whether the ponds be used for rearing fish or for sporting purposes, or for both, the advantage of this arrangement is obvious, for should one or two very large fish remain in a pond after it has, presumably, been cleared, or should a few of them grow considerably faster than the others—as is very frequently, indeed most often, the case—they will assuredly

PONDS ON A STREAM.

prey upon the new stock introduced for rearing purposes, or the old stock retained for sporting purposes. One or two only of these older and bigger fish among a large number of smaller ones spells disaster; for all trout are more or less cannibals, and unless the fish in the pond—especially for rearing purposes—are a pretty " level " lot in size, the smaller specimens are sure to pay the penalty for their unfortunate backwardness in growth. A judicious " sorting " and the removal of any very large fish, therefore, becomes advisable from time to time.

Before proceeding further, I would like to make very clear a point that has just occurred to me, and, consequently, may also have occurred to the reader. I do not advocate bringing the whole of our British waters under complete artificial control—even if such a thing were possible. I am far too keen an angler myself to dream even of a state of affairs that would result in you and me knowing exactly what size fish we should meet with in this or that water. I would not—if I could—rob my brethren of the angle—and myself!—of the glorious uncertainty of capturing a two-pounder within a few yards of where we have just hooked and returned a small fish of perhaps not more than a quarter of a pound. Let the cultivation of such waters be limited to the proper protection of the redds and an occasional "stocking" when necessary. But we must have ponds under complete control, or protected portions of rivers, if we are to rear fish for stocking these wild, fascinating waters with their little one here and their big one there a few yards away. Moreover, if I have made me a pond or two in mine only meadow, I want those ponds to hold as good a head of fish as possible; therefore, a pretty level lot becomes a necessity.

In Fig. 7 A is the pond, formed by banking up and damming back the stream at B B; the dotted lines C C show the original bed of the stream in what is now the pond, and D is the course of the stream below; at E E are horizontal box screens (to be described presently); F is the controlling sluice for regulating the height of water in the pond, and emptying it; and G is an underground drain, through which passes the surplus water to a convenient point and level below. Of course, the drain may leave the pond at any convenient point, not necessarily as shown.

In Fig. 8 we are still in "meadow-land," and I suppose a series of ponds required on a limited length of stream, where the fall is not sufficient to permit of a simple arrangement like that of "lakes in the hills," to be described presently, yet they are required to be—independently and collectively—under complete control. In the drawing, A, B, C are a pond and the lower and upper parts of two other ponds; the dotted lines D D D show the original bed of the brook; E E and E are controlling sluices; and F F F F F is the underground

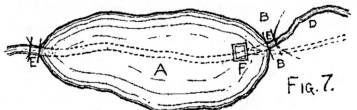

Fig. 7.—Plan of a Pond on a Stream.

drain, by means of which the water from the sluices is carried off. In putting in this drain, be sure of your levels, and see that there is a good fall from E to F and from E E to F, and so on through the series of ponds. At G G and G are horizontal box screens; H, J, L, and M are adjustable sluices; K, K, K is a surface surplus water channel, which also acts as a supply channel when any of the ponds are being lowered, and thus keeps a constant supply of water running through those ponds not to be operated upon.

By supposing K, K, K to be an existing stream, the drawing becomes a plan of ponds formed off a stream. In the drawing

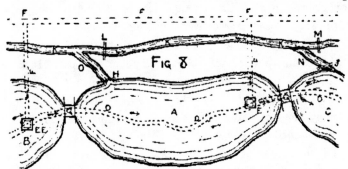

Fig. 8.—Plan of a Series of Ponds on a Stream in a Flat Country.

I have shown the surplus water channel and the surplus water drain on the same bank, but this need not be so; indeed, where circumstances are favourable, they are better kept on opposite banks.

Let us suppose that pond A is to be emptied, and that ponds B and C remain full (or nearly so) with water running into and out of them continually while operations are going forward in pond A. Sluice H is adjusted so that no water can enter from the surplus water channel K K K. Sluice L is adjusted so that the water has free access down the channel K K K. Sluice M is adjusted so that a sufficiency of water is diverted into the branch channel N, and so into the pond C, by way of sluice J. Lower the height of water in pond B by means of the sluice E E four inches, or even six, so that no water flows through the screen G. Now empty your pond A at the sluice E. While the operations in pond A are going forward, the water is flowing from the channel K K K into the pond C over the sluice J. Should there be a shortage of water in the channel K K K, it is remedied in the following manner:—Pond B has a similar branch channel to O, in connection with A, and N, in connection with C, and a similar sluice to those at H and at J. Adjust this sluice so that the top board is slightly lower than the top board at sluice E E; the surplus water, instead of flowing down the controlling sluice E E, falls over the sluice at the branch channel, and so joins, and adds to, the volume of water flowing down the channel K K K. But if your levels are right and your sluices in the channel properly adjusted, this shortage of water will not occur.

Several little matters that may, perhaps, puzzle you now will be made quite clear in the chapter on "Sluices." It may be thought that the method of handling the ponds is complicated and expensive, but when you learn how simply and cheaply the apparatus is made and fixed any such idea will be abandoned at once.

The next photographs illustrate the method of forming ponds in a hilly district; the sheets of water, indeed, are of such proud proportions that they are entitled to the term of lakes, especially the lower one, of which I managed to get a decent view. The problem in this case was quite a common one. In a very hilly district, amid grouse moors and rabbit warrens, a stream tumbled noisily down a rocky gorge be-

tween steep banks on either side. Here and there was a
decent pool, that held a few tiny troutlings, and at a few
places a hole held a half-pounder; the stream could not
be expected to hold anything more important. At times
it was a rushing torrent, and the obstacles to the formation
of anything in the shape of a fish-pond under at all decent
control seemed to be almost insurmountable. Yet to-day that

DAM AND SURPLUS WATER CHANNEL IN THE HILLS.

gorge is occupied by a splendid series of ponds, which contain
some thumping trout, for the sale of which the proprietor
(Mr. C. W. Wilson, of Rigmaden Park, Kirkby-Lonsdale, .
Westmorland, who, by-the-bye, is a good man to call in should
any help or further advice be necessary in connection with
the formation of lakes in hilly districts) could quite easily
get a handsome return for his money. At the same time, he
is the happy owner of a valuable fishery, where before existed
only a noisy stream.

Fig. 9 shows "how it is done." The drawing is a plan of

one lake of the series. Each lake can be emptied at will, and each has its range of redds, but these are used by the proprietor only as a means of gaining possession of the fish at spawning time, as they are spawned by hand, and the ova incubated in a hatchery elsewhere on the estate. I need only add that in the drawing the lake and dam are out of all proportion, so far as size is concerned, to the rest of the details. This is rendered necessary by the fact that otherwise a large space would be occupied to no purpose.

SAME, LOWER DOWN THE VALLEY.

A is the lake, formed by damming back the stream at B B. Two things command especial attention in connection with the construction of a dam—first, the diverting of the course of the stream, if at all possible, while the work is going forward; second, the material. Now, in this case the material was close by, but it had to be dug and quarried. Having in mind also the two essentials of an effective trout pond—complete control, and disposal of surplus and flood water—all four conditions are realised, and the problem of the formation of the ponds is solved by cutting a surplus water channel, K J K.

on the side of the gorge down which the stream flowed.   Into this channel the stream is diverted from the top end of the gorge while the dams are being constructed, and communicating channels are cut, as at H, as the work advances.   The materials obtained in cutting these channels are utilised in the construction of the dam, and the channels now are used to carry off surplus and flood water.   At M is a sluice to control the passage of water from the pond into the channel H; the redds are at G G G; and F is the stream below.   Now, in this

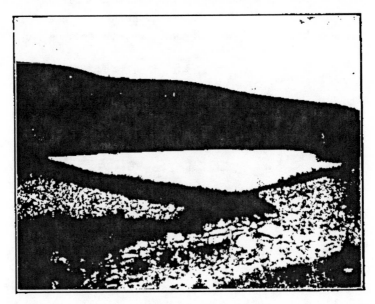

A LAKE IN THE HILLS.

case the fall is so great that the bottom of the pond A at its deepest part is above the level of the stream F below; and it is the same case with the remainder of the series of lakes.   To empty it or to adjust the water in it to any height, therefore, simply means the placing of a controlling sluice at D, connected with a drain (shown by the dotted lines at E), passing through the bottom level of the dam and discharging its contents into the stream F below.   The controlling sluice D and the sluice M are really all that is necessary to control the lake; but, to make assurance doubly sure, a horizontal box screen is fixed

at the top of the dam at c, and the top sluice board in the
controlling sluice D is so adjusted that, under normal conditions, about three inches of water are flowing into the horizontal box screen at c and over the sluice at M. It is pretty
plain that each of the three outlets assists the other two, and
that in combination they quite control the water passing
through the ponds. Any surface water that may enter the
ponds is really beneficial, as it goes to form a useful spate
without any fear of flooding. I think that, with the help of
the photographs, all other matters are made quite clear. I
may add that where room is of consequence the redds, G G G,

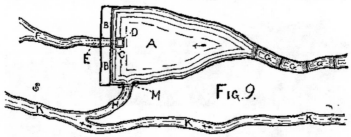

Fig. 9.—Plan of a Lake in the Hills.

may be made in serpentine form, and thus a larger area of
spawning ground is obtained in the same distance.

If you wish to make a set of fish-ponds in which trout-rear-
ing may be carried forward under the most advantageous circumstances, then you must choose a favourable position, similar
to that which forms the subject of the four next illustrations,
and the set of rearing ponds must be made off the main
stream. The accompanying plan (Fig. 10) shows you how to
go about the work, and I may say at once that a fishery so
planned is the most simple and perfect that present
knowledge of pisciculture permits; indeed, I fail to see how it
can possibly be improved upon. Also, the scheme can be
curtailed or extended; the planning of the fishery still remains perfect; only, if more ponds are required, other distributing ponds should be made. A greater number of rearing
ponds to each distributing pond than is shown in the plan is
not advisable.

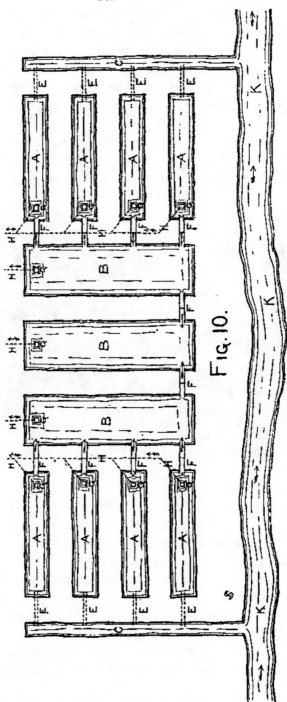

Fig. 10.—Plan of a Set of Rearing Ponds.

Only a very few words of explanation are necessary. ᴋ ᴋ ᴋ is the main supply stream, which is "tapped" at either end of the fishery, where distributing ponds, ᴄ ᴄ, are dug at right angles to the stream. These distributing ponds are kept filled with a plentiful supply of water from the stream. The water is conducted from them into the yearling ponds —which are marked ᴀ—by means of underground channels—marked ᴇ—which are described in my remarks on making artificial redds off a stream, and illustrated in

A DISTRIBUTING POND.

Fig. 4 and Fig. 5. Note that the ponds ᴀ are at right angles to the ponds ᴄ and the ponds ʙ, and that each of the ponds ᴀ receives an independent supply of water—an important matter, and one that is only too frequently overlooked.

The water passes from the yearling ponds ᴀ through horizontal box screens—marked ꜰ—and so into the two-year-old ponds, marked ʙ. Thus, each of the outside two ponds, ʙ, receives the whole of the water supply from ponds ᴀ, and each of these supplies has passed through one yearling pond only. The whole of the water supply to the fishery finds its way from the two outside ponds B, through horizontal box screens F, and into the centre pond B.

The height of water in the ponds is regulated, and they are emptied at will—each independently, in sections, or the whole of them at one time—by means of the controlling sluices, marked G, which communicate with underground drains shown by the dotted lines H.

I think the drawings and photographs go to prove that it is

A SET OF REARING PONDS.

quite a mistake to associate the formation of a fish-farm with the construction of expensive rearing ponds fitted with complicated apparatus.

The illustrations are from photographs of the Earl of Denbigh's fishery, at Ysceifiog, North Wales, which has been formed recently under the superintendence of Mr. J. B. Feilding, from plans submitted by Herr S. Jaffe, of Osnabruck, Hanover.

Before I pass from the subject of ponds and lakes, there are two or three little matters you may as well know. And the first of these is the best method of digging a pond.

If you really mean business in connection with your rearing
ponds—and I presume that you do—it is as well to dig them
direct from the soil. It is a golden rule to do so when they
are formed off a stream. Cement sides and bottoms to a rearing pond are a mistake. The only material that may be used
with safety, other than mother earth, is wood; and where
the soil is of such a tricky nature that some support becomes
necessary, stout planking, well charred and carefully covered

CONTROLLING SLUICES IN PONDS.

with black varnish, answers the purpose admirably, and plank-
lined ponds may well rank next to those dug direct from the
soil. My next illustration is of a typical rearing pond, at the
Earl of Denbigh's fishery, Holywell, North Wales, and
Fig. 11 shows a simple method of digging such a pond.
I have purposely omitted the inlets and outlets, including the
controlling sluice, as these are dealt with fully in another chapter, and I wish to keep the instructions for digging a pond outside the pale of the slightest complication. Fig. 11, then,
shows the way of digging a pond after an approved manner.
A is a cross-section at the deepest end of the pond;

B B is a section through the length of the pond, and it is purposely broken at c to avoid the drawing taking up space to no purpose. The sides and ends of a pond should be dug at an angle of 45deg. to the plane of the surface of the water, and there should be a shelf, D, about eight inches wide and four inches from the top of the soil, E, which materially guards against the washing away of the bank from the incessant action of the water, and is other-

OUTLETS FROM HORIZONTAL BOX SCREENS.

wise useful. Pond A should be at least one-third shallower, and it may be even less than half at the inlet end than it is at the outlet end, which should be the deepest part, if only to facilitate the handling of the controlling sluice. The sides, ends, and bottom may be puddled, if necessary, or they may be lined with planks, as already stated, but the natural soil is best. A convenient size for a yearling pond is 50ft. by 10ft. Never get your ponds—for rearing purposes—too large. The depth of a pond depends upon its situation and the average temperature of the water in it. What you have to guard against is your ponds "warming up" in summer time; there-

fore, if at all exposed to the rays of the sun, with no counter-
acting influence such as plenty of shade from trees, or water
that runs at a very low temperature, even in summer time,
they should present as little surface to the action of the sun

A REARING POND.

as possible, i.e., they should be deep and narrow. Shade may,
and should be, supplied by the growth of aquatic plants, and
by placing shading screens at intervals across the pond (see
chapter on "Rearing Fry and Yearlings"); but depth and
narrowness are the great preventives of your pond warming

up to a disastrous degree of temperature. A good workable depth for a pond 50ft. by 10ft. is 18in. at the shallow end to 4ft. 6in. at the deep end, and it may well be that the width of the pond should be considerably decreased before the depth is increased to any very great extent, even at the expense of having the sides at a more vertical angle than is advisable under normal favourable circumstances.

It is always a nuisance and the source of continual trouble— and often expense—when ponds are formed above the level of the surrounding countryside. I do not recommend their construction under such circumstances. Still, I have seen ponds successfully formed so; and the next illustration (turf-sided ponds) illustrates the best method I know of .

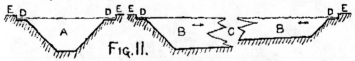

Fig. 11.—Section of a Rearing Pond.

in this connection. I photographed these ponds while they were in course of construction, at Mr. C. Braun's fishery, at Sowley, Lymington, Hants, in order that the method of their formation should be made quite plain. The sides are formed, in the first place, from ordinary turf, cut from the surface of the adjoining meadow-land, and then piled one turf top of another, until the desired height is reached, in the manner shown. Afterwards soil is heaped against the outside until a long, shelving bank is formed. Other soil is heaped inside, so that the ponds assume the shape as in Fig. 11. They are then puddled, and form very decent rearing ponds—of their sort.

Should a pond become very foul from any cause—and where constant care is not exercised this is very likely to occur—take no half-measures. Lower the water out and give the bottom and sides a plentiful dressing of lime, as shown in the next illustration. Then let the pond lie fallow for two, three, or even four months, and fill up again, being very careful not to let any of the surplus water escape to any other pond below. Run plenty of water through the pond and down the controlling sluice for a month, and then have a fresh start. Neglect or want of precaution render the liming of some ponds necessary, and, as I have said, if it must be done, then 'tis as well it should be done thoroughly. But prevention, in this, as in most other cases, is better than cure; therefore, avoid the fouling of your ponds from whatever cause arising. And this is generally a somewhat simple matter.

TURF-SIDED PONDS.

My remarks concerning the formation of ponds and lakes would be quite incomplete without some reference to the oldest form of artificial water in this country. I allude to a moat. In less peaceful times than these, moats were formed, in a great measure, for the protection and isolation of the building they surrounded. But, even in those days, during a temporary cessation of hostilities, their value as fish-preserves was recognised and considerably enhanced by simple methods of cultivation. With the advent of modern methods and improved apparatus they become—where they still exist—most valuable sheets of water, more especially because they are quite easily brought under control. Where they do not exist, and the contour of the ground permits it, one may quite easily do worse than form them; and the instructions I have already given are sufficient for the work.

It may be rank heresy on my part, but, all the same, I should like to see a lot of existing moats entirely cleared of their present stock of coarse fish, proper sluices and screens put up, and the water then judiciously stocked with a suitable variety of Salmonidæ. I can quite easily imagine the dogged

METHOD OF LIMING A POND.

opposition such an idea as this will meet with in certain quarters; but the fact remans that, in my opinion—and I am not alone in such opinion—where coarse fish can be supplanted by Salmonidæ, they should be, whether it be for sporting or food purposes. Utilise all the coarse-fish water you can for cultivation of Salmonidæ, and there will still be ample left for the followers of coarse-fish angling. Moreover, these coarse-fishermen will quickly learn to place at its right value the enhanced condition of angling as a sport, and, needless to say, their wives, or their cooks, will appreciate the vast improvement of the quarry from a culinary point of view. Partly through prejudice, but principally through apathy, fishing for trout is an unknown or little exercised sport in many districts throughout England, yet in most cases the methods of attaining it would be quite simple.

These matters, however, are hardly within the scope of my present discourse. I will return to my legitimate subject. The two next illustrations are of an artificial moat and a sporting water formed off it. As a matter of fact, the moat

AN ARTIFICIAL MOAT.

itself is an excellent sporting water; but the proprietor very wisely uses it principally as a rearing water from which many other waters are annually stocked. If he wishes to give his friends " a treat," however, they are permitted to fish the moat, and you can easily imagine the result, for it is literally full of splendid trout! There is no need for me to give a plan of this water; the photographs speak for themselves, and, of course, you quite understand that proper sluices and screens are erected at all necessary points. I only need add that here is another case of a prolific and picturesque water formed where once flowed only a brook. Note, also, there is plenty of shade. The proprietor does not mind the extra trouble with fallen leaves; he knows so well the value of shade.

And now just a few concluding remarks, and I have finished with the formation of ponds and lakes. Where you have no fear from flood, a surplus water channel is only necessary if the fall in the ground does not permit of any other means of lowering the ponds right out, and then it takes the form of what I have termed a surplus water drain, in order to distinguish the latter from a surface channel. This, I hope, is made perfectly clear in the drawings. But where a flood is probable be sure to have your surplus water channel of sufficient dimensions to carry off quite easily the greatest volume of water that is at all likely to come down. If your ponds are in a position much exposed to the sun in summer time, keep them as deep as possible. Under any circumstances, grow plenty of aquatic plants of the right variety—of which more in the proper place. In the case of making use of an existing pond and improving it after the manner I have shown, be sure of the history of that pond before you start the work. If there are no fish in it, find out why before you start to stock it, for the latter, from unalterable circumstances, may be an impossibility. When starting to make a pond, be sure you have fixed on the most suitable situation possible, and make sure of your levels to begin with. You need not necessarily make a pond just off a stream or river; more favourable conditions may exist half a mile away, and it may be better to cut a supply channel that distance, especially as this channel may be utilised for supplying fry and yearling ponds en route. By an exercise of some common sense in this connection much time and money may be saved. Here, perhaps, a dam, sluice, or screen can be erected with most satisfactory results, and with the minimum amount of expense; a little further on the result would probably be quite different. Don't expect water to run up hill! Give as much fall as possible from pond to pond where you form a series of them, and be sure that your surplus water channels and surplus water drains have plenty of fall.

If, in digging your ponds, you should run against and open out any springs, make use of them by all means, but carefully mark their position and guard against them forming a lurking hole for enemies to your stock. If necessary at any time, do not hesitate to lower the water to examine them and make them safe.

I would emphasise the fact that when you empty your rearing ponds for the purpose of obtaining or sorting the stock, be sure that all the fish are cleared out; let there be no nook or

A SPORTING POOL OFF THE MOAT.

cranny beyond control where a big trout may remain to play havoc with the new stock to be reared. At the same time, you may advantageously have "lurking" spots in your ponds, for trout like them; but locate each one, and look to it carefully before you refill your pond to re-commence rearing operations.

The water supply and the necessary aeration of it is specially dealt with in a separate chapter, as it need be.

Just one other point. If you are not quite sure of overcoming your difficulties before you start on the formation of

E

ponds or lakes, do not hesitate to call in the assistance of an expert in the beginning. You will probably be well repaid for the small outlay incurred in connection with the payment of his fee for advising you.

The illustrations are from photographs of the moat and pool below the moat at Weston Hall, near Norwich—the home, in Norfolk, of Colonel F. H. Custance.

CHAPTER IV.

SCREENS AND SLUICES.

The importance of properly constructing screens and sluices and most carefully fixing them cannot be over-estimated. To a very large extent the success of your operations depends upon proper control of the water supply, and this control occurs principally in connection with the screens and sluices. And the first word of advice I shall give you about them is, Avoid complicated apparatus; let your arrangement cf screens and sluices be as simple as possible, so long as it is effective, and let them be substantially put into position

A screen should not receive the current, and, consequently, the debris brought down by it, "full face," unless it is absolutely unavoidable. Screens should either slant up from the bottom to the top, away from the current, or they should be placed at an acute and obtuse angle—not right angle—across the stream. Sluices should invariably be arranged so that the water is drawn off from the surface, otherwise difficulties are bound to crop up. These are the two principal matters to bear in mind; but other minor points arise in connection with the erection of sluices and screens, and these are dealt with, as they occur, in the following description of approved apparatus.

The first illustration in connection with this subject is a photograph of a controlling sluice as fixed in a pond, and in the illustration the pond is empty. Figs. 12, 13, and 14 are sections of the contrivance, which has for its object the adjustment of the water in a pond any height and the emptying of the pond at will. Fig. 12 is a sectional elevation of the sluice through a line A B (i.e., from back to front, centrally), marked in Fig. 13, which is a sectional plan of the contrivance through

A CONTROLLING SLUICE FIXED IN AN EMPTY POND.

a line C D, marked on Fig. 12. Fig. 14 is a section through a line E F in Fig. 12. The sluices are made and fixed after the following manner:—

Three stout boards, marked G, are firmly fixed together in

the form of an elongated box, without ends or top, two boards forming the sides and the third the bottom. The length of these boards is one foot more than the deepest part of the pond from B to H, Fig. 12, at which point the contrivance is erected. At one end is formed a strong flange, J, which at

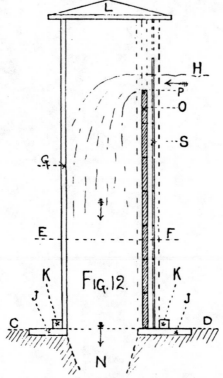

Fig. 12.—Sectional Elevation of Controlling Sluice.

the front is wider than at the sides or back, in order to permit of the sluice boards and screens falling on it when in position. This flange is strengthened and more firmly attached to the boards by means of the second flange, formed from square wood, marked K. At the other end is fitted a detachable cap, marked L, Fig. 12. Next the contrivance is fitted with three long strips of wood on each side and inside. These are marked M in Figs. 13 and 14, and their relative position in Fig. 12 is shown by the upright dotted lines parallel with

the sluice boards and screens. These strips go to form two
grooves, one inside the other, throughout the entire length of
the contrivance. Now let us stand the sluice upright and in
position as shown in the photograph and in Fig. 12, and firmly
fix the flange J to the bottom of the pond immediately over
the outlet N, Fig. 12, which is in communication with the
surplus water drain so often referred to in my plans of the
various ponds. The flange is preferably seated on brickwork
or cement concrete, to which it can be bolted by plugs let into
the brickwork or concrete, and fitted with screw ends and
nuts. What was the uncovered top of our imaginary elongated box thus becomes the open front of the sluice. Next
the cap, L, is removed, and a number of sluice boards, marked

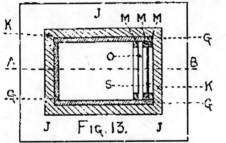
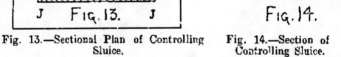

Fig. 13.—Sectional Plan of Controlling
Sluice.

Fig. 14.—Section of
Controlling Sluice.

o in each drawing, are slipped down the inner groove until
the sluice is filled with them to the desired height, which in
Fig. 12 is marked P. These boards govern the height of
water in the pond, for it is above the top edge of the top
board—P, in Fig. 12—whatever number of boards may be in
place. It is equally evident that when all the boards are removed there remains nothing to prevent the whole of the
water escaping into the drain N. But the apparatus is not
complete yet. It becomes necessary to guard against any
debris escaping down the sluice and so rendering the surplus
water drain liable to become choked; and, what is even
more important, the fish must be prevented from escaping in
the same direction. Now comes the use of the other grooves,
down which are slid a number of perforated zinc screens,

marked s, in all three drawings, in front of the sluice boards, and so arranged that the top screen reaches at least a foot above the top edge of the top sluice board. Of course, the water now has to pass through the screen before escaping over the sluice board, and down the surplus water drain. Put the cap in position once more, and the controlling sluice is complete. The real simplicity of it is best realised in Fig. 14. When lowerin~ the pond, release one sluice board at a time,

INLET OF A HORIZONTAL BOX SCREEN.

and always keep the screens well above the last board removed. Each board may be fitted with a small screw-eye; they are then quite easily removed by a hand hook. Char the wood inside and out, and cover well with black varnish before placing the sluice in position. For ordinary ponds up to, say, six or seven feet in depth, these sluices need only be made of wood, but, in the case of very big lakes, and where they have to control a very large volume of water, they are preferably built up from brickwork, and strong iron gratings take the place of the perforated zinc screens. Otherwise the planning of them is the same, and the method of working does not differ in any case.

The controlling sluice illustrated is built from a model by Herr S. Jaffe, and is in use at the Earl of Denbigh's fishery, at Ysceifiog, North Wales.

One of the most simple screens to place at the inlet and out-let of a pond, and, in conjunction with the controlling sluice just described, one of the most effective, is what I have styled a horizontal box screen, and it forms the subject of the next illustration.   Fig. 15 is a sectional plan of the apparatus

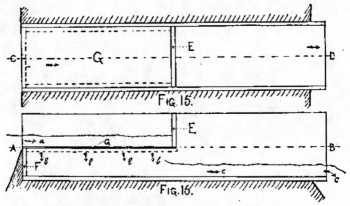

Fig. 15.—Sectional Plan of Horizontal Screen.

Fig. 16.—Section of Horizontal Screen.

through a line A B of Fig. 16, and Fig. 16 is a section through a line C D of Fig. 15.   I think the present photograph and drawings, together with the photographs that accompany Fig. 10, make the use of this screen quite clear.   It is formed after the following very simple manner :—Two sides and the bottom only of a long box, made from stout boards.   Midway is placed a partition E, which extends from side to side and half the depth of the box from the top edge.   At the inlet end another similar partition occurs, F, only in this case it extends from side to side, half way up from the bottom.   Throughout half the length of the box a perforated zinc screen, G, extends, and this is fixed to the two partitions E and F, and further sup-ported by strips of wood fastened lengthwise on the sides of

the box, and by cross bearers from side to side if necessary.
This screen, or rather parts of it, may be so fitted that they can
be removed if necessary, i.e., just lifted out; and perhaps this
is advisable more often than not. The box is fixed in the
bank of the pond, so that the screen at the inlet end is about
three or four inches below the normal height of the water in
the pond, which is adjusted, as I have said, by the controlling

AN OUTLET SHELF OR LIP.

sluice. When the box extends from pond to pond, as in Fig.
10, the outlet end should project into the pond somewhat, so as
to throw the water well out into the pond in order to guard
against washing away the shelving bank; or, better still, an
outlet shelf or lip may be attached to it, as shown in the
illustration. By-the-bye, this outlet shelf or lip is advisedly
placed at any description of outlet, for reasons which will
become obvious as we go forward with our operations. In
action the water enters the apparatus at the arrow a, falls

through the screen G, in the direction of the arrows, b b b b, and flows out of the apparatus in the direction of the arrows c c, either into the next pond or into a surplus water channel. Any debris is left on the top of the screen G and removed by an assistant when necessary. The screen does not often require cleaning, as the debris is carried against the partition E, where it accumulates, leaving the greater portion of the surface of the screen quite clear. It will at once appear clear that no fish can pass this box screen either up or down. Of course, it cannot be used to empty a pond. It is not intended for that

AN OVERHEAD HORIZONTAL BOX SCREEN.

purpose, and is, preferably, used in connection with a controlling sluice. The inside and outside and all fittings should be charred and covered with black varnish before being put into position.

The illustration of an overhead horizontal box screen is a photograph of a most useful contrivance for supplying water absolutely free from debris to fry ponds. The system here shown keeps all debris on the move, and, properly set up, in the manner now described. it should work without choking for months. It is in the form of a long trough, and two inches above the bottom of this trough a false bottom of perforated zinc runs the entire length. Holes are made in the wooden bottom of the trough, and at the bottom of the front side at

both ends of the trough, to draw off one-fifth of the quantity
of water passing over the screen, i.e., the perforated zinc
bottom of the trough. The remaining four-fifths of the water
is conducted by an extension of the trough to a surplus water
channel, and carries with it all debris. The trough is fixed
level, but the channel from which it gets its water supply
should have a fall, and should for preference run at right
angles to the trough at the intake. This supply channel is not
shown in the illustration, nor is the extended end of the
trough leading to the surplus water channel. The lengths of
perforated zinc forming the false bottom are fixed on a cleat
fastened against the side of and all along the bottom
of the trough. The illustration is so perfectly clear and so
easily understood that a drawing of a section is quite unnecessary.

The horizontal box screen illustrated is made from another
model by Herr S. Jaffe, and is in use at the Earl of Denbigh's fishery, Ysceifiog, North Wales; the outlet shelf is
in use at Col. Custance's Weston Fishery, Norwich; the overhead horizontal box screen at Mr. Edgar V. Corrie's Itchen
River Trout Breeding Establishment, Winchester, Hants.

A form of screen that is very much in favour with many fish-
culturists is known as the slanting screen, and it is generally
used in combination with an ordinary upright sluice. The
next photograph is a general view of the contrivance as in use
at Mr. H. H. Gray's Hyde End Fishery, Brimpton, Berks,
and Figs. 17 and 18 are a section and sectional plan of same.
Where one pond only is concerned, this contrivance, by being
made sufficiently deep, can be used for emptying the pond
and for adjusting the height of the water without the assistance of a controlling sluice. It is a useful sluice and screen to
use at D, in Fig. 2 and Fig. 3 (see chapter on Redds), and in
similar positions. It is very simple, but needs putting up
strongly. The bottom, on line A B, in Fig. 17, must especially
be made sound or the water will work under the sluice. This
slanting screen and sluice may also be formed in a box after
a similar manner to the horizontal box screen, or the hori-

zontal box screen may have strengthening sides, as shown at
c, in Fig. 18. The reason why the slanting screen should
generally be made with the strengthening sides is that it is
much deeper in any case than the horizontal screen. In the
drawings E are strongly framed sides of wood, or they may be
built up of brickwork or concrete; D is the slanting screen,

A SLANTING SCREEN.

which rests on a strong framework of wood; and c are the
sluice boards, manipulated in exactly the same manner as
those in connection with the controlling sluice. The
arrows show the direction of the current. The water
passes between the sides E, through the screen D, over the
adjustable sluice boards c, and so into the next pond or into
the surplus water channel.

The next photograph is of part of a big screen across the

river Itchen, at Mr. E. Valentine Corrie's trout breeding establishment, Winchester, Hants, and it quite clearly illustrates
the structure, the plans or drawings of which would be quite
useless unless they were of a most complete character; hence
I think it inadvisable to give any. To a piscicultural engineer

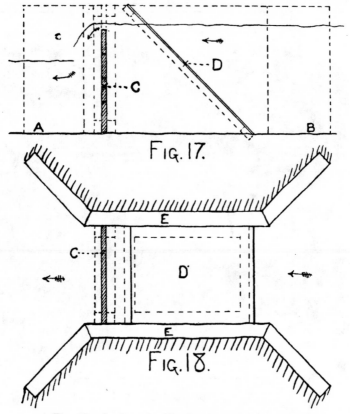

Fig. 17.—Section of a Slanting Screen and Sluice.

Fig. 18.—Sectional Plan of Slanting Screen and Sluice.

or to a properly qualified workman the photograph is sufficient
to show the sort of thing that is most suitable. To all others
concerned I would say, Do not attempt the construction of
these very big screens yourself; call in the advice of an expert,
and in this connection you cannot do better than consult Mr.
E. Valentine Corrie; he has built up some of the very best

PART OF A BIG RIVER SCREEN.

and biggest screens in this country, and I have never known him to make an indifferent job of any of them.

But there is a simple yet important matter in connection with the construction of these big river screens that may well be referred to and illustrated, if only because it embodies a principle which applies to all screens, little or big. And this is the correct angle a screen should assume across a river. I have had occasion already to point out that the wrong way to put up a screen is at right angles to the banks. The correct way is shown in Fig. 19. A is the screen, placed at an obtuse

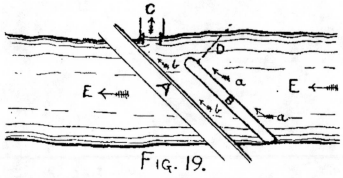

Fig. 19.—Plan of Arrangement of River Screen.

and acute angle across the stream; B is a plank—or, for preference, a strong fir-pole—moored partly across the stream by means of a chain, D, and kept parallel, or nearly so, to the screen. The direction of the current is shown by the arrows, E E. Any debris coming down stream, especially heavy, floating weed, etc., strikes against B, and is naturally drawn in the direction shown by the small arrows, a a; that which escapes under the pole or plank B finds its way to the screen A, but here again is drawn in the direction of the small arrows, b b; only the water flows freely through all in the direction of the arrows, E E. At c a channel is cut and a sluice put up. The channel may lead to a surplus water channel or into another stream, or it may join the main river at a convenient point below. This arrangement has been shown again and again in previous drawings. When a mass of debris has accumulated in the corner where the screen A forms an acute angle with the bank at the sluice c, all that has to be done is to raise the sluice, and the consequent rush of water carries all the debris down the waste channel. In action a screen thus formed almost clears itself automatically, and the little debris that does cling to it is easily removed by an attendant, as shown in the photograph. I think it will be easily realised how much better it is to erect a screen after this manner than to adopt the orthodox plan of placing it at right angles to the banks, with the inevitable result that all debris coming down stream is forced against it, very quickly chokes it, and in the end the great pressure of debris may result in the destruction of the screen, or, at least, serious injury to it.

I cannot too strongly impress upon my readers the importance of constructing all screens and sluices in a thoroughly substantial manner, and from the very best materials obtainable. I have already referred to the importance of fixing them securely. If the greatest possible care is not exercised in this connection, disastrous results may very easily follow, and then it may cost pounds and a loss of much valuable time to put things right—even if that be possible. True economy lies in the employment of best materials and workmanship. When possible, the stream should be diverted while the work goes forward, and the water should not be permitted to flow through or over the structure until all is complete, and, in the case of cement or brick-work, not until the materials are thoroughly "set" and hardened. The framework of a screen should penetrate well into the banks on either side, and into the bottom of the stream. Any neglect of this will surely result in a tiny escape of water to commence with and ultimately the undermining of the whole structure. Moreover, the very object of the screen—the prevention of fish escaping—is quite unattainable unless the whole structure is "tight" and sound. Should any leakage occur after all possible precautions have been taken, there is only one thing to be done; no half-measures are of the slightest use. The pond must be run dry, or the course of the stream again diverted, and the faulty work put into thorough repair. But the golden rule is to make assurance doubly sure in the first place; for it must not be forgotten that where disaster occurs not only is work-manship destroyed, but, in many cases, the stock of fish is lost also, only be regained at considerable expense, and certainly at great loss of time. A free flow of water through a screen is a sine qua non. Hence it follows that where much debris comes down a river a pair of screens (one much coarser than

FRY ENCLOSURES FORMED OFF A BROOK.

the other) is an advantage. So far as the material from which they should be made is concerned, a great deal depends upon the size of the screen. Where a somewhat broad river is screened off into sections, upright bars firmly riveted into stout iron frames is the approved method; or a stout frame-work of wood may be covered by an approved size of galvanized upright wire screens, as shown in the photograph of the Itchen river screen. But when the work is of less importance in size, stout, perforated zinc is generally used. The objection to perforated zinc is the need of frequent renewal, but this, after all, is merely a minor matter, and the expense is not

F

much.   Do not, however, neglect this necessary renewal, or one day your fish will escape, and the painstaking of many months will be rendered futile.

Ascertain the very highest flood level and construct your screens and sluices in accordance with the requirements of the situation.   As I have already pointed out, the great consideration is the choice of position for your ponds or screened portions of stream or river; but when every care has been taken in this connection there still remains to exercise some fore-

FRY ENCLOSURES FORMED ON A BROOK.

thought concerning the screens and sluices, or the whole of your work may one day be submerged, if not actually washed away.   Carry all your work well above the highest point reached by the biggest flood, and have ample room—depth especially—in your surplus water channels, and all should be secure.   Make sure that your screens are sufficiently large to permit of the greatest possible push of water passing safely through them.   Keep your screens of uniform size, and always have a few spare ones in stock of different size perforations. The value of this advice cannot well be over-estimated.

Having erected the screens and sluices after an approved

manner, insist—personally—on proper attention being paid to
their working. It is an astounding fact that most attendants
are neglectful of screens and sluices, although in many cases
they are quite conversant with the enormous importance of
the proper working of them.

In the chapter on natural and artificial redds I have referred
to the importance of using screens for protective purposes, and
in dealing with the rearing of fry I have occasion to allude to
ths usefulness of specially screened portions of a stream or
specially fenced-off fry enclosures. The screens used for these
purposes need not necessarily extend the whole width of the
stream. Fig. 20 shows an elevation of an approved style of
screen for a fry enclosure, and the accompanying photographs
illustrate the application of the same to fry ponds and also to a
stream in which fry are being reared. The photographs were
taken at Mr. E. Valentine Corrie's fishery, and that gentleman was kind enough to remove some of the screens in order
to show how the fry are permitted to have the full range of
several fenced portions of a brook as they advance in growth.
In other cases the screens remain in position. It will be noticed that in each case the screens are fixed at an acute and
obtuse angle across the brook or at the outlet of the fry pond,
exactly after the same manner as that adopted for the big
river screen, and with exactly the same objects. In Fig. 20,
A A is a strong framework of wood covered with stout planking,
and B is the screen (which may also have a set of sluice boards
in front of it, if necessary, as in Figs. 17 and 18), and the
lines c c c c show the outline of the bank and bed of the
stream. All the framework beyond this is buried in the bank
and in the bottom of the stream. Of course, the lines c c c c
may be extended as far as necessary on either side
and below, but the framework also should be proportionately extended, as the secret of stability lies in this
penetrating well into the bed of the stream and the banks.
The screen apertures must be made to take screens of varying
perforations, and this remark, by-the-bye, may well be applied
to all framework for screens.

In conclusion, I would remind you that all woodwork used in connection with screens and sluices should be thoroughly charred and well varnished before being put into position,

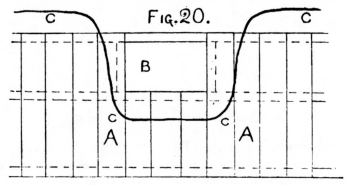

Fig. 20.—Elevation of Screen for Fry Enclosure.

and, if necessary, should be periodically attended to in a similar manner.

CHAPTER V.

WATER SUPPLY AND AERATION.

Throughout my discourse I am endeavouring to keep a direct line of argument and to give attention to matters in their

WATER SUPPLY AT HOWIETOUN, ABOVE.

proper priority and natural sequence. But where all matters are nearly, if not quite, of equal importance, this is a path very difficult to pursue, even if it be possible to do so at all. For instance, the water supply and the natural or artificial aeration of it may well claim to be of first importance to the fish-culturist; and because I have first dealt with the formation of redds and lakes and described the apparatus connected with their construction, it must not be thought that I have lost sight of the vast importance of the present subject.

As a matter of fact, a fishery without a proper water supply would be like the play of "Hamlet" with the Prince of Denmark left out. I would go even further, and assert that the water supply is the heart's blood of the whole concern. I credit it with so much importance, indeed, that I recommend a proper chemical analysis of it being made before it is used for fish-farming purposes, even though the supply be copious and to all appearances perfectly pure. More than one fish-farm in this country—and in others—has come to grief from lack of water or from impurity of the supply. Therefore, where you are not absolutely assured of the purity and volume of your water supply do not attempt the construction of a fishery.

Some waters that are admirably suited to the requirements of incubation are absolutely useless for rearing purposes. But these may be made suitable after the manner to be presently described. It may be taken for granted that a water rich in natural food is to be preferred for ponds, etc., while that direct from a spring of almost perfect purity is best for incubation. I have previously pointed out that temperature has much to do with successful fish-farming, and I only refer to it here again in order to emphasise the fact that it should guide you in a choice of water supply. But do not condemn a water supply that "warms up" in summer time until you have exhausted the possibilities of shading by means of planting trees or other methods referred to elsewhere ; for many of these " warm " waters are rich in natural food. And it must not be forgotten that rainbow trout can be reared in water of much higher temperature than can brown trout, and I am quite convinced of the usefulness of rainbow trout in this country if they be planted under proper conditions.

Where it is possible to store your water, in order to guard against a shortage in summer time, do so by all means ; and in this connection mill-heads and lakes in high altitudes are often invaluable adjuncts to a successful fish-farm. But pure spring water may be utilised if it is first run in the open for some considerable distance, and preferably through watercress beds. Mr. Wilson, of Rigmaden Fishery, can vouch for the great value of running the supply to rearing ponds through other ponds or parts of the stream planted with watercress. On his farm he has established a system of alternating watercress ponds with ponds containing fish, and to this he attributes—

WATER SUPPLY AT HOWIETOUN, BELOW.

correctly, I believe—the splendid condition of his stock of rainbow and other trout.

Of equal importance to a copious and pure supply of water is its proper aeration. The late Sir James Maitland realised this when he utilised the Loch Coulter Burn for the supply to his famous fishery at Howietoun. I give two illustrations of this supply, one above and one below the bridge at Milnehome hatching-house, in order that you may see what a perfectly aerated supply should be like; and the nearer your supply reaches this perfection the more successful will be your operations. But it does not fall to the lot of all of us to have such a perfect supply; therefore, we must content ourselves with

something as near to it as possible; and it is comforting to
know that we can help Nature a lot in this connection.

I think it is a pretty well established fact that trout will
thrive in a higher temperature of well aerated water than they
will in sluggish water. For instance, in a well aerated water
Fario have been known to successfully battle with a temperature of 70deg. and even more, while a sluggish water at 60deg.
will sicken them and 70deg. may prove fatal. Add at least
another 10deg. in each case where rainbows are reared, and we
get a range of over 15deg. in favour of well aerated water, and
this often means the difference between success and disaster.
This is why I have continually impressed upon my readers the
importance of having good falls where possible. It is also
advisable to " break up " the water supply as much as possible
before it enters into the rearing ponds or fenced-off portions of
a stream or river. In the case where the supply is taken
from a stream this can easily be done by placing large stones
or boulders in the bed of the stream, and by the formation of a
series of small pools and succession of falls. Mr. Wilson
adopts a capital method of aerating water as it passes from
pond to pond. He places a sheet of perforated zinc parallel
with the surface of the water and through this the water falls
and is " broken up " after a very simple manner. This screen,
of which I give a photograph, is also a capital barrier against
fish mounting up from the pond below. The same gentleman
has devised a most ingenious method of aeration, where only a
very slight fall is obtainable, and this contrivance is shown in
Fig. 21. A is a dam that heads back the supply of water from
the stream, which passes into the pond through a six-inch
pipe, B B. An inch or inch-and-a-quarter pipe, C, is fixed well
above the water level, and carried into the pipe B. The rush
of water through the pipe B automatically draws with it a large
and constant supply of air through the pipe C, and this is
forced into the volume of water flowing into the six-inch pipe
at D and so into the pond E. Simple as this contrivance is, it
is most effective, and ensures a plentiful aeration—considerably more than occurs in the case of an ordinary fall of water.

I strongly recommend the contrivance wherever a slight fall only occurs from pond to pond, or from supply to first pond. It may be used separately or in conjunction with an ordinary fall.

The chemical analysis that I have recommended should be—if favourable—sufficient guarantee of the suitability of the water supply; but a few hints concerning this may not be out of place. Even in the neighbourhood of limestone or iron caution should be exercised. That trout live in such districts

AN AERATING GRATING.

goes beyond saying; but the formation of a fish-farm, at which the most favourable conditions should, if possible, exist, is quite another matter. Pollution from lead ore or "blend" spells failure in all cases. Other pollutions to be especially avoided are those resulting from gas-works, distilleries, tanneries, and some descriptions of paper-mills. It is foolish to form a fishery in the neighbourhood of any of these or of similar industries.

A low temperature water produces hardier brown trout. This fact should always be taken into consideration where choice of water supply is concerned. On the other hand, rain-

bows would appear to thrive best—in this country, at least
—in a higher temperature, more especially if the water is productive of much natural food, as high temperature waters
generally are.

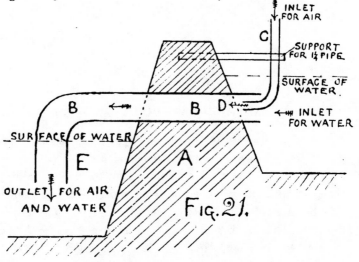

Fig. 21.—Section of Aerating Contrivance.

Should your water supply be derived entirely from springs
close by, then you may make it more suitable before it enters
your fishery by running it through serpentine channels, which
may be planted with watercress here and there and formed
into " broken water " after a similar manner to that recommended for a natural stream.   By running through serpentine
channels the water covers more ground, which is just what
is wanted.

CHAPTER VI.

NATURAL FOOD: AQUATIC PLANTS, ETC.

Having made sure of the water supply, and having completed the construction of your ponds or fenced off portions of river or stream, the next care is to look to the larder, i.e., attention must be given to the food supply and the proper establishment of aquatic plants, etc.; indeed, the planting of the latter should, in some cases, go hand in hand with the work of construction. Perhaps Dame Nature has lavished favours on you in this connection, and, if so, so much the better. In the matter of some sporting waters, where a good and, seemingly, plentiful supply of natural food exisits, it is as well to make quite sure of this before introducing the maximum stock of fish that the water could and should carry. Very often it will be found advisable to increase the quantity. And that which is advisable in the case of sporting waters becomes absolutely necessary in that of ponds and sections of river or stream used for rearing large numbers of fish. In addition, natural food has, in most cases, to be supplemented by artificial feeding, of which more in another place.

Absolutely barren waters are by no means rare, and it is simply absurd to stock these with fish. But they can in many cases be made into useful waters; and where this is possible it should be done. The marvellous thing to me is that some owners of waters—otherwise absolutely sane men—will plump a number of fish into an absolutely barren water and expect them to live and thrive! As well expect sheep to fatten on the wooden roads of London streets! Food, and plenty of it, and of the right sort, is absolutely necessary to fish life; without it, fish-farming operations spell failure. And not only do the fish require food, but that food itself requires food. Hence it follows that a good larder must be kept, and grazing ground provided for the filling of it. And this brings us to the subject of aquatic plants.

Aquatic plants have many uses on a fish farm. They not only form natural preserves in which the food of trout can be produced in enormous quantities, but they also provide shade and shelter for the fish, and, in many cases, are invaluable in connection with the maintenance of a plentiful supply of oxygen in the water; for all aquatic plants, more or less, consume carbon gas, which, if present in sufficient quantity in any water, spells death to all trout. Moreover, in the process of consuming carbon they set free oxygen, and thus provide fish life with an increased quantity of that life-giving element.

Without hesitation I place the common watercress (Nasturtium officinale) in the premier position of all aquatic plants on fish-farms. The value of its presence in large quantities cannot be over-estimated. Useful everywhere, it is invaluable in the stream that supplies the fishery with water; in the distributing ponds at the head of the rearing ponds and redds; on the redds; and at the shallow parts and edges of the ponds; in the fenced potions of river or stream, and in special ponds alternating with rearing ponds or redds. Water benefits immensely by passing through beds of watercress; young fry delight in the shelter it provides, and thrive on the large quantities of food inevitably associated with its growth; and mature fish profit by its presence in a proportionate manner. So very useful is this plant that I recommend its introduction wherever possible. On the banks of some big, deep rivers, unsuitable in themselves for the promotion of its growth, suitable ponds for its reception may be made, and a sufficiency of water permitted to flow from the river, through the watercress bed, and into the river below, with marked beneficial results. That the fish appreciate the presence of these beds of cress is amply proved by the fact that they congregate at the outlet awaiting the food that is brought down, and the otherwise enriched water that is found there.

Valuable as watercress is in fish-culture operations, it is not all-sufficient, if only for the reason that it will not grow in deep water. Moreover, we must not overlook the fact that in some cases it cannot be grown at all, although these latter are, fortunately, very few and far between. In my estimation, the plant that ranks next to watercress in importance is lakewort (Littorella lacustris), and where the two can be established in conjunction your stock of natural food—for young fish especially—is pretty well assured. Lakewort fills the gap left by watercress, inasmuch as it is admirably adapted for the bottoms of ponds or lakes. It ranges in height of growth from two inches to four or five inches; in exceptional cases I have seen it as high as seven or eight inches, never more. The free growth of lakewort ensures an enormous supply of small mollusca and valuable animalculæ, and, in common with watercress, it never becomes a nuisance from overgrowth. It is a good tip to establish lakewort in your ponds before starting to fill them with water, and afterwards to replant patches of the bottom that may, perhaps, become bare Once established, only ordinary care is required to ensure a permanent covering for the bottom of your ponds.

Other suitable plants to encourage the increase of mollusca, crustacea, and numerous animalculæ are: Water lobelia (Lobelia dortmanna), Marsh marigold (Caliha palustris), water plantain (Alisma plantago), dwarf spearwort (Ranunculus flammula), starwort (Chara flexilis), and water moss (Fontinalis antipyretica). Of these, water lobelia will sometimes flourish where lakewort will not, and vice versa. They are very similar plants in growth, only that lobelia flowers and may be established by means of seed. If both do well in your water, so much the better. The marsh marigold is suitable only for the edges of ponds and for shallow waters. It is a capital plant for artificial and natural redds and for any waters in which very young fish are being reared. In some cases water plantain is apt to grow too freely, but where this is the case it is easily stopped if taken in time. Otherwise it is a most useful plant, more especially for providing shade and shelter for the fish. It will grow in water varying from one foot to four feet in depth, and about two feet of water seem to bring it to best perfection. Dwarf spearwort is another plant with fine, sheltering leaves, which gracefully float on the surface. This plant does best in not more than two feet of water. It is a capital plant for fry ponds. The two last, starwort and water moss, are both useful in streams or ponds through which there is a rapid current, and in which the other plants mentioned are less suitable, even if at all possible.

The larger growing aquatic plants may be objected to in rearing ponds pure and simple, yet they cause but little extra trouble when lowering the ponds for the purpose of netting the fish, and one is well repaid for this extra trouble by their presence. They are not only very useful, but in many cases they are very ornamental as well. There should always exist a sufficiency of them in sporting waters. Principal among these are the water lily, of which I prefer the white species (Nymphœa alba). It is not quite so coarse growing as the yellow (Nuphar lutea). The yellow, however, may be planted in very large lakes or ponds. There are several species of imported lilies that do fairly well, but for all practical purposes the above two are sufficient. The yellow iris (Iris pseud acorus) might well be planted in far greater quantities than it is, and numerous imported varieties lend a charm to the banks and the stream sides. Then there is, of course, the common bulrush (Typha latifolia) and the much smaller bulrush (Typha augustifolia). Another of the rushes that I feared had left us, but which has come to the front again of late, is the flowering rush (Butomus umbellatus).

Great caution should be exercised in connection with the introduction of plants into a stream or pond. You will be quite safe with those I have recommended, but there are two, at least, that I wish to caution you against. For, whatever the advantage of their presence may be, I am quite sure it in no way compensates for the trouble they cause. The first, and worst, of these nuisances is water milfoil (Myriophyllum) and the other is a gift from our American cousins, and known in this country as the American weed (Anacharis alsinastrum). I have heard of cases in which waters have benefited by the introduction of either or both of these, but in the whole course of my travels I have never met with one. On the other hand, I have seen scores of waters literally choked by their rank growth, and it would appear to me that where they get the upper hand—and this is pretty well always the case—there is no remedy but running the pond dry and letting it remain so for two or even more years, during which time grass may be established on the bottom of the pond, and this, together with the establishment of some of the plants recommended, should benefit the water considerably and most probably get rid of the nuisance. But prevention is better than cure. So do not be tempted to introduce either of the plants condemned. Should they exist already in a fishery, make it your business to get rid of them without delay.

If it is most inconvenient—perhaps impossible—to empty the ponds, then uproot as much as you can of the plaguey stuff before it starts seeding, and take great care that the weed so uprooted is carted away and either buried or burnt. In this way you may manage to keep it under control, but you will not get rid of it entirely.

There is a useful weed, which requires cautious handling; that is, the common pond weed (Potamogeton); and, from an angler's point of view, this weed is a capital addition to a sporting water. It must, however, be kept under control and not permitted to seed. And in this case you are well rewarded for your trouble, for big fish delight in the cover provided for them after this manner.

The usefulness of the common reed (Arundo phragmitis) needs only passing reference. And now for a few general remarks in connection with the establishment of aquatic plants in angling and fish-rearing waters.

It must not be forgotten that the great object of weed

planting in a fishery is to bring about a plentiful supply of natural food, without which it is quite impossible to breed and rear trout. Some waters are, naturally, stocked with plenty of aquatic plants; others, especially newly-formed ponds and lakes, require to be planted; and I would again emphasise the importance of doing this, in the first place, before the ponds are filled with water. It may happen—does happen frequently—that a newly formed pond provides an enormous store of food for the first year or two, without the introduction of aquatic plants at all. But this is merely a temporary source of food, which is, comparatively speaking, soon exhausted. But while it is being exhausted is the very time that the aquatic plants should be establishing themselves; they will never have such another chance of doing so. Therefore, plant early and plant thoroughly. Be sure that every plant is well " set." One plant properly put into the soil is worth a score put in anyhow.

The importance of arriving at and maintaining a correct balance of animal and vegetable life in your ponds, streams, or rivers cannot be over estimated. There is no royal road to this, but the rich reward amply repays for all time and trouble taken, and in many cases it depends as much upon the absence of certain plants as it does upon the presence of others. Therefore, do not introduce plants other than those I have recommended, unless you are an authority yourself or have consulted an authority on the subject.

Always thoroughly overhaul the stock of plant life and animal life existing in a water into which you propose to introduce trout; and let this be done before they are introduced. This often becomes necessary even in the case of ponds that have been specially made. And in this connection arises another great usefulness of having your ponds quite under control, as I have instructed all the way through. The water in them may be lowered, or they may be run dry, as the necessity of the case compels. But do not make the mistake of running your ponds dry, or for that matter materially reducing the depth of water in them, at any time unless it is absolutely necessary, for you are sure to lose more or less quantities of natural food, however careful you may be. In the case of fry-ponds, the depth is necessarily adjusted—for rearing purposes—from time to time; but, as this means an increase of depth, not decrease, the objection does not obtain.

You may very well devote some of your spare time to studying the life history of many of the microscopical inhabitants of your ponds and streams. Such knowledge is especially useful in connection with rearing very young fry after a natural manner, and it is a fascinating subject.

As with land plants, so with aquatic plants: Certain soils suit certain species and not others. When possible, plant that which naturally takes to the soil, but should the soil be unfavourable to all alike, then mix with it a sufficient quantity of suitable soil obtained from elsewhere. With some of the larger plants it is as well to dig in a little stable manure, well rotted. This is especially the case with water lilies. Set your plants only as few hours as possible before the water rises and covers their roots. All planting is best done in the spring. Do not make the great mistake of thinking that when the aquatic plants are set all that is necessary has been done. They require, and should receive, constant attention Treat the bottoms of your ponds or streams as you would a kitchen or flower garden, and all will go well.

While I am dealing with planting I may as well have a few words to say about suitable trees and shrubs for the banks. As I have already pointed out, these, for several reasons, should be in evidence in sufficient numbers at every fishery. I do not forget there are ways of doing without them; but experience goes to prove that they are extremely useful if not absolutely necessary. Here again, then, where planting has to be done, we want to establish those which encourage insect life; and of these I prefer, in their order of merit, alder, oak, and willow. Almost any shrubs, many tall growing plants, and the hardier sorts of dahlias, are all useful. The grass, excepting on the actual pathways, may well be permitted to grow long and thus harbour innumerable insects which in large numbers alight on the water. G

Having established the aquatic plants, you may with safety introduce any quantity of the various species of mollusca, and take care they are always present in sufficient quantities to satisfy your stock of fish, but not in such bulk—in sporting waters, at any rate—as to satiate the trout so that they do not seek other—preferably surface—food.   Most of the crustaceans are also safe, but some of them are parasites of an objectionable nature, and, careful as you may be, they at times attack your stock of fish, with unfortunate results.   The remedy for this evil is simple—a strong bath of rock-salt in solution—but the bother and trouble of catching the fish and bathing them is most annoying.   In the fry-ponds and the stream that feeds them, establish an ample supply of daphniæ, cyclops, and cypris—all commonly classed as "water fleas" : they form invaluable food for the fry.   They can be obtained from Mr. W. Baily, of the Malvern Wells Fishery.

In this connection a matter of importance occurs : Wherever a strong flow of well aerated water passes over the fish, these parasites seldom trouble them. Another matter, and one which I cannot explain, but can vouch for, is that wherever fresh water shrimps (Gammarus pulex) are introduced in large quantities, these parasites give considerably less trouble.

The larvæ of nearly all the water flies can be obtained now, and these certainly should be introduced where possible.   Mr. E. Valentine Corrie, of Winchester, sends out large quantities of these larvæ, and the Solway Fishery Co., Dumfries, and Mr. C W. Wilson, of Rigmaden Fishery, can supply you with all the most suitable aquatic plants

CHAPTER VII.

STOCKING.

In my introductory remarks I have pointed out that the delicate processes of spawning fish, incubating eggs, and rearing very young fry need not necessarily form part of the operations undertaken by the amateur fish-culturist in the early stages of his work. But as the proprietor of a water, who has so far followed my instructions, should now be possessed of a suitable home for trout, it remains for him to stock it. Therefore, I leave the explanation of the operations referred to above for the present, and deal with the subject of stocking with fish or eggs which have been advanced beyond these delicate stages by a commercial fish-culturist.

Many proprietors of fisheries who stock artificially prefer buying from a fish-farm to breeding and rearing themselves. For my own part, I am inclined to think that by so doing they miss the most fascinating operations connected with the improvement of a fishery; but I cannot go so far as to say that they—or, at least, all of them—are entirely wrong. Spawning, incubation, and the early stages of rearing are not such difficult matters to-day as they were a decade ago. Big strides have been made in the simplification of the necessary apparatus and the handling of it. Hence we are learning that even the most delicate operations in connection with fish-culture are not beyond the common sense of an ordinarily intelligent man or woman; and I include woman with very good reason, for, strange as it may appear to be, on the biggest commercial fish-farms their careful manipulation of eggs, their regular and painstaking methods of feeding the fry, and. beyond everything else, their willingness to act according to the instructions of the expert in charge of affairs, instead of adopting methods of their own, as male assistants are, unfortunately, apt to do, have resulted in the employment of women in preference to men in numerous cases. But, still, the fact remains that in some cases it is cheaper and better to purchase stock than to breed it, this being so especially in cases where the number of fish required is small, or sport is wanted at once, and the owner of the water has not yet realised the possibilities of breeding a stock of fish for himself and others at the same time.

Be the reason whatever it may, I will suppose for my present purpose that a fishery has been made, and that it has no inhabitants other than those that go to form food for the trout that are to be introduced. It may happen that you have a decent stock of fish already; if so, let well alone for a while, and see what you can do with those you have after the various methods of cultivation presently described. But I will deal with a fishless water. By-the-bye, let me also make it quite clear to my readers that these present remarks apply to stocking with the common brown trout of the British Isles (Salmo fario). Stocking with other varieties is treated separately in another chapter.

The most simple method of stocking is to purchase a number of yearlings from the nearest commercial fish-farm, place them in lake, or pond, or fenced-off portion of river or stream, and carry them forward to the two-year-old stage, when, if they have had a proper supply of natural food and have further benefited by judicious artificial feeding as well, they should be ready for the rod or for the market. This form of fish-farming may be indulged in with successful results, without any knowledge beyond that possessed by the average angler. And it pays—financially. Moreover, it is a good way of starting fish-culture operations, and is sure to whet the appetite for more serious work. I have already explained how the necessary precaution should be taken for the protection of these fish; it only remains for me to say, in this place, that they should be introduced into the water if possible during the winter time, or, at any rate, not later than March. After that they have started to feed freely on the fish-farm whence they come, and, for this and other reasons, are less likely to travel without injury. Such injury, I may add, is not always evident on their arrival at their new home; but it has occurred, none the less.

It is quite common knowledge nowadays that fish should not be transferred direct from the water in which they have travelled into the water they are intended to stock. The two waters should be gradually assimilated in temperature by the repeated addition of some of the lake or stream water to that in the fish carriers until that in the carriers has been raised to the same temperature as that in the lake or stream. I say raised, because, probably, the temperature in the carriers will be lower than that of the water of the fishes' new home. But it may be higher, although, except during a very severe frost, it should not be. During a very severe frost it is inadvisable to introduce fish. This objection does not occur in connection with what I may term "frosty" weather, which is excellent for travelling fish. One other hint: Purchase the yearlings from a farm on wh'ch you absolutely know there is a plentiful supply of natural food; and do not make the mistake of thinking that because a yearling trout is not six inches long it is less valuable for stocking purposes. It may quite easily be far more valuable, as I point out in my remarks on artificial feeding.

Next to stocking with yearlings, the simplest plan is to "sow" fully-eyed ova on natural or artificial redds, where they exist, or where they have been formed and properly protected after the manner I describe in the chapter on that subject. I would repeat here that I consider this to be one of the most effective and most economical methods of stocking waters for sporting purposes. In the chapter referred to, I have dealt fully with the manner in which these redds are utilised where a stock of spawners exists. Now I propose to deal with manipulation of them where there are no spawners, my remarks being intended to supplement those already made. By fully-eyed ova is meant eggs which have passed through the early and middle stages of incubation in a properly constructed hatchery, and are " sown " on the redds when they are within a few days of hatching. All that is necessary is to rake level a part, or parts, of the redd, or redds, of sufficient size to receive the ova easily. Of course, I presume that no predatory fish are on the redds, and that the protecting screens are in their place below (see Figs. 2, 3, and 6). The eggs may be transferred from the box in which they have travelled, or from the trays in one's own hatchery, direct to the redds. As a rule, it is not advisable to sow more than five hundred fully-eyed eggs in one " nest," and care should be taken that none of them touches another. A fairly sharp, but by no means rough, current of water is best, and, if at all possible, choose a spot free from the risk of a dangerous amount of sediment accumulating. It is advisable to protect the eggs—and the alevins and fry later on—under any circumstances, by the erection of tanned netting screens or light galvanized wire netting screens, as explained in Chapter 2. If you have any real cause for fearing danger from birds or animals, such screens become an absolute necessity. I have already told you to make sure about the quality of the eggs, but I repeat the caution. Your fully-eyed eggs should hatch before any harm can come to them. As soon as the bulk of them have hatched out, run a little extra water over the alevins. You will notice the little fish will " pack " together in masses. This is as it should be ; it is a sure sign they are healthy. After hatching, all that you can do for the next two, or perhaps three, weeks is to look to the water supply and keep the enemies of the alevins at bay.

As soon as the little fish have lost the umbilical sac (see chapter on rearing fry) they will commence to feed, and should the redds hold a sufficiency of natural food they will look after themselves. But artificial feeding, in addition, may be advisable, and this process is explained in its proper place.

When the fry are three months old the fine perforation screens may be changed for others of coarser perforation, so as to permit of the young fry leaving the redds at will, while still preventing larger fish getting on the redds. A large number of the fry will avail themselves of the opportunity to leave the redds and seek a living elsewhere, and thus they will gradually populate the adjacent waters in communication with the redds. If too many remain behind after June, a lot of them may be carefully netted out and transferred to suitable quarters in any waters close by that it is wished to stock. In August you may take the screen away to let any fish that choose have access to the redds; but by this time your stock of fry on them should be as small as possible. Thereafter the conduct of the redds I have already instructed you in. You will be fortunate if you rear twenty-five per cent. of fry from the alevins to the six-months stage. This percentage will cost considerably less than purchasing six-months fry, and certainly they will be more valuable fish, seeing that they have been actually hatched and reared in the water in which they have to live. In concluding this portion of my subject, I again impress upon you the importance of providing plenty of shade for the young fish.

You may purchase fry and stock with them. But I cannot see where the advantage of " planting " fry over " sowing" ova comes in; and I certainly know of a lot of disadvantages. First, there is the difficulty of travelling fish at the time of year when fry are fit to move. If you stock with alevins this objection does not obtain; but, again, I ask, Wherein lies the superiority of these over fully-eyed ova? Secondly, I maintain that you cannot expect fry to do so well if planted as fry as those reared from ova sowed on redds, seeing that the latter are hatched in the water they are to live in—a consideration to which I lend much importance. I have known it to mean the difference between success and failure. I admit the probability of a loss in the alevin stage, and even a big loss in the early fry stage; but consider the very large number of eggs you can sow at the cost of a few thousand fry delivered to your fishery. The item of carriage alone of fry as compared with carriage of eggs is an important one. Only in the case of having a hatchery and fry ponds of your own, and these close by or actually on the water to be stocked, do I consider stocking with fry to be as valuable as sowing fully-eyed ova; even then the "planting" must be very carefully done. However, you may stock with fry, especially if it happens that you have no suitable redds—properly protected—on which to sow eggs, and are, therefore, compelled to resort to either fry or yearlings.

But in this connection an important matter crops up. Different waters, or different portions of the same fishery, vary considerably in depth, and the deeper the water to be stocked the older the fry must be. This matter I deal with fully in my remarks on rearing fry, and before stocking with them you should refer to that chapter as well as this. This is where the enormous value of a hatchery and fry ponds attached to a fishery comes in. From them you can stock with fully-eyed ova, and then, in due season, first the shallows can be treated with young fry; next the slightly deeper parts can receive three-months fry; after this the deep, slow water can be stocked with six-months fry; and, finally, the remainder of your fish in the rearing ponds may be cleared out and planted in the fishery as yearlings. And while your fishery has been in a continual state of receiving stock, your rearing ponds have been prevented from becoming overcrowded.

Mr. E. Valentine Corrie is a firm believer in stocking with fry, and in his hands several fisheries have been enormously benefited after this manner. He goes so far as to assert that in the case of some waters it is far and away the best method of stocking, if persistently and thoroughly done. His experience of one water in particular is exceptionally interesting. It was a neglected river, in which pike and other coarse fish had been permitted to get the upper hand. It is to-day a prolific trout stream. And this change has been brought about principally by planting fry. Of course, pike were netted out each year, and so gradually reduced in numbers, but long before any appreciable inroad was made into their ranks plenty of trout were caught, and those of a takable size. At the present time the trout have got the upper hand; and this has been the case for some years back. The piece of water referred to was a two-mile length of river (similar, I may say, to such a river as the Itchen), and when taken in hand in 1880 it was almost bare of trout, and was swarming with pike of all sizes up to 17lb. in weight. The few trout that were in the water were too "pike scared" to rise, and were useless for sporting purposes. The first season's fishing (including netting) resulted in the capture of seven very big trout, and 1,304 pike. The same season the first lots of fry were planted. Next season (1881) 52 trout were caught and 936 pike. In 1882, 132 trout were captured and between 700 and 800 pike; the exact number of pike was, unfortunately, not entered this year. In 1883, 250 trout and 400 pike were taken from the water. Season 1884 saw the capture of 361 trout and 450 pike. After this the number of pike rapidly decreased, and the number of trout reached up to as many as 500 in one season. This truly marvellous improvement in the fishery becomes even more remarkable when one learns that the captured trout averaged 1¼lb. in weight! In 1884, 300 eight-inch trout and a few hundred yearlings were turned down, with a view of introducing new blood; but the whole of the former never grew to killable size (one pound weight), probably owing to their being either stunted two-year-olds, or possibly they were raised from immature stock fish. All the stocking from 1880 to 1885 (inclusive), with the exception of these fish, was done with fry! The fry were hatched from ova of wild fish, pure Fario, and they were planted at proper ages to suit varying depths of water and other circumstances. I am delighted to give publicity to this work of Mr. Corrie's, and also to the following very strong support of my theory re the value of artificial redds, etc.:—

"To improve existing natural redds is, of course, possible," says Mr. Corrie, "but small artificial redds formed off a river must succeed if properly laid out where the nature of the

ground permits of the necessary fall or gradient. My success at
trout farming is chiefly due to artificial redds. Yet they cost almost nothing.   They have never failed wherever I have known
them to be made, and two or three are capable of stocking miles
of water, turning out from 15,000 to 20,000 fry per mile if
dealing with a big water."

I could point to several cases in which attempts have been
made to stock rivers and streams with yearlings and two-year-
olds, and the results have been anything but satisfactory. The
same water, when stocked with fully-eyed ova and fry in
various stages of growth, have done well.   I hope it will not be
thought that I am advocating stocking with fully-eyed ova and
fry, those and only those; I am merely endeavouring—not
without some hope of success—to encourage these simple
methods, being convinced that if more attention were given
to them the result would be most encouraging; and, what is
more, they would be permanent.

In another chapter I allude to several methods of rearing fry
by the side of a sporting water before they are permitted to
enter the latter.   In passing I may refer to the folly of purchasing fry and transferring them direct to an open water on
which no pretence of protection whatever has been made.

You may stock your redds, and therefrom your fishery, by
the introduction of spawners to your fishery, but in this case
I must again caution you against the folly of introducing un-
healthy or otherwise unsuitable fish to your fishery.   As to
choice of spawners, see my remarks on spawning fish.

If a pond, lake, river, or stream is to be stocked with a view
of affording sport at once, then two-year-olds may be introduced.   Such waters should only be stocked in late autumn,
winter, or early spring; otherwise the fish may suffer in travelling and from preparation for travelling; and, although
they may appear to be in good health on arrival, they may
quite easily have become almost impossible for sport—at least,
for that season.   For preference, spring is the best time for
stocking; the newly introduced fish have then a far better
chance of getting an ample supply of natural food.

Whether the fish be fry, yearlings, two-year-olds, or older fish, they must be quietly and gently introduced, never "chucked" in. It is a good thing, where possible, to entirely sink the carrier, and gradually "float" the fish out. Do not handle the fish unless absolutely necessary.

CHAPTER VIII.

RAINBOW, AND OTHER FOREIGN TROUT.

I think this a convenient opportunity for dealing with the matter of introducing rainbow trout, Salmo irideus, and other foreign trout into British waters. I have previously explained the necessity of exercising caution when introducing any trout other than the brown trout of this country into any new waters or into any waters in which it is proposed to increase the stock of sporting fish. It must not be thought from this that I am against the introduction of foreign trout; nothing of the kind. As a matter of fact, I am a strong advocate of stocking suitable waters with rainbows, but only suitable waters; and, this being so, it is as well that I should give some opinion as to what I consider are suitable waters.

There is little or no doubt that the introduction of foreign trout into our waters received a well-deserved check through the injudicious planting of Salvelinus fontinalis some years ago. This fish, which is generally known as the American brook trout, and was accepted in this country as a trout, is really a char, and one of the best and handsomest of all the chars. It is indigenous to those regions lying east of the Allegheny Mountains and the Great Lake district extending from Georgia on the south to Labrador on the north. In America they have been widely distributed by artificial introduction and have done remarkably well in many States, including Nebraska, Colorado, Nevada, and California. English fish-culturists and fishery owners were much impressed by their

beauty and seeming suitability to our waters. Had they
tested the matter thoroughly all would have been well, for,
without doubt, certain British waters would profit by their introduction. But they were distributed over the country,
utterly regardless of whether or not the water in which they
were planted was suited to their welfare. The inevitable
result followed. Taken all in all, they did more harm than
good, and in the end were voted a failure, notwithstanding
the strenuous efforts of a few prominent fish-culturists who
knew their value under proper conditions.

Now, as a matter of fact, Fontinalis delights in clear, cold
mountain streams and lakes of low temperature. A water
that warms up to anything much over 60deg. means the deci-
mation of a stock of Fontinalis, if not, indeed, their total
destruction. In their native country they leave the streams
in hot weather and seek shelter in deep parts of the lakes; and
they only thrive where these lakes are available, or, of course,
where the mountain streams do not warm up. With these
facts before us we can account for the failure of their attempted introduction into the bulk of British waters where
they were planted. They might have done well in some of
our mountain streams and lakes, but they were planted in
wrong positions to begin with; they were a failure in those
positions. This failure gave them a bad name, and, with very
few exceptions, British fishery owners will have nothing to do
with them now.

I do not think our fisheries lost much by this failure, and
certainly our fishery-owners, and not a few fish-culturists,
learned a lesson in stocking that has stood them in good stead
since. The pity of it is that a creditable carefulness has in
some cases degenerated into extreme prejudice against the introduction of any foreign fish whatsoever, with the result that
at one time we were very near condemning rainbow trout,
whereas time has proved that caution only is necessary.

But before I proceed to discuss why and where I think rainbows should be introduced, I would express the emphatic
opinion that wherever brown trout will thrive, they—

and only they—should be planted. I do not make this assertion idly. I have made most careful inquiries, and have personally visited fisheries and fish-farms all over the United
Kingdom, and it has always been my most earnest effort to
ascertain, and where possible to see for myself, the conditions
under which certain fish thrive and others do not. It is a
complex matter, but not beyond solving. At least, we may
take it for granted that in many cases where only troutlings
are found in a water the remedy lies rather in the introduction
of more food into such water than in an ill-considered scheme
of stocking with some other variety of trout. The judicious
introduction of new blood—i.e., brown trout from some other
British water—is at times advisable, but more often it is
merely a matter of food. It is quite possible also that a water
may be over-stocked, and, if so, the fish are sure to degenerate
in size and condition. In such a case the remedy is obvious.
I think I am right in asserting that the brown trout proper
(Salmo fario) has reached a higher stage of perfection in this
country than in any other. It is one of the noblest of game
fishes, and as a surface feeder it has no peer. This latter fact
alone should, and does, endear it to every British angler, and,
therefore, I repeat, wherever it will thrive there it should be
encouraged; and, what is more, the variety should be kept as
pure as possible. But, after the whole of the suitable waters
in the British Isles have been stocked with British trout,
there will still remain many thousands of acres of water in
which they will not " do "; and where it is possible to populate
these waters with some other variety of Salmonidæ the work
should be done. In my concluding remarks on the formation
of ponds and lakes, I express the opinion that many coarse fish
waters in this country could be stocked with rainbow trout,
and I give my reasons for thinking why it should be done. I
repeat the opinion here in order to remind my readers that
much water lies to their hand which might be improved without any interference with the stock of brown trout in the
country, and there would still remain ample for coarse-fishing
purposes.

In its native home, which extends from California, near the Mexican boundary, to Southern Alaska, the rainbow trout (Salmo irideus) is found to thrive in a wider range of temperature than any other of the Salmonidæ. The habitat of the fish is by no means limited to slow, deep, and warm-running rivers, although it seems to "do" better in this country in such. It is this adaptability to a high or low temperature of water that has made the planting of rainbows in this country not only possible but actually profitable—from a fish-farming as well as a sporting point of view. And it is the fact that they will stand a much higher temperature than the brown trout that has made it possible to stock with rainbow trout where the introduction of brown trout is impossible. In big rivers and lakes they do well side by side with Fario, and, in the case of really big waters, I see no objection to their introduction. By a big river I mean such as the Thames, the Trent, or the Lea. They would certainly thrive in such rivers as the Itchen, the Test, the Darenth, the Derwent, the Coquet, and other similar waters, but only at the expense of Fario, and, therefore, their introduction to such waters would be unwise. Lakes and reservoirs certainly profit from their introduction, especially where the former have feeders up which the fish can mount at spawning time; or redds can be made after the manner I have already described. Rainbows are easily reared, and, granted two conditions—first, plenty of food; secondly, plenty of shade—they well repay cultivation. The condition of shade may arise from depth of water, or from trees or aquatic plants; but it is most important that it should exist, otherwise ophthalmic troubles occur, with the result that the fish have trouble in finding their food, and, consequently, fall off in condition very rapidly. Rainbows hold their own in coarse-fish waters containing pike and perch, but under these circumstances it is advisable they should have plenty of range. Where waters communicate with the sea, rainbows will migrate, but, apparently, only when a lack of food occurs in the waters in which they are introduced. For my own part, I cannot see any particular objection to the development of this migratory instinct. They are pretty sure to return to their old quarters in due season, and their journey seawards has made them much bigger, hand-somer, and more valuable fish. The rainbow trout matures at the third year, but it is of most value for spawning purposes from the fourth to the seventh year. Some little difficulty occurs in connection with its spawning season, seeing that it spawns after the brown trout and before the coarse fish. But this, after all, is a minor matter that is easily dealt with. It is stated that in some cases the rain-bows are assimilating their spawning time to that of our brown trout, but I have found no actual evidence of this. Certainly, some of them spawn earlier than others, but this is the case with brown trout also. Attempts have been made to cross Irideus with Fario. What is to be gained should such a cross succeed I quite fail to see; but so far I believe it to have failed, for the reason given above, i.e., the difference in the time of spawning, although it might be possible to cross a very late Fario with a very early Irideus. Summed up, the rainbows would thrive in most of our British waters, but it is inadvsable to introduce them—with the ex-ceptions mentioned above—where brown trout are doing well. They should be introduced where Fario does not thrive, and should be planted in coarse-fish waters wherever possible. They must have plenty of food; rainbows would starve on the allowance that brown trout will do quite well with. They are very game fish, and rise freely to the fly, but would seem to prefer "fancy" patterns rather than the orthodox duns, gnats, and spinners. This is another reason why they should not be introduced side by side with Fario in a dry-fly fishing stream, although they might ultimately settle down to an Itchen or Test diet, for they have already developed a pen-chant for Mayflies! What trout would not?

Just a word or two concerning Levenensis, Loch Leven trout. A feeling is rapidly spreading that these are no more nor less than Fario. This much is certain : That at the year-ling stage they are hardly—if at all—distinguishable one from the other. In some waters where they have been introduced the third, and even the second, generation has found them most astoundingly like the trout indigenous to that water. For the most part the parent fish retain their characteristics, but the progeny certainly do not. For this reason I see no particular value in Levenensis other than as valuable and safe " new blood " in streams, or for stocking waters of similar character to Loch Leven.

With reference to Bavarian great lake trout, Alpine char, and other foreign fish with which certain British fish-culturists are experimenting, I would strongly advise the exercise of considerable caution in connection with the introduction of them into any waters in this country until we know more about them. Mayhap we shall have other valuable additions to the stock of game fish in our waters from among them. But, whilst guarding against prejudice, let us be cautious. And these remarks apply equally to the introduction of any foreign trout either at the present time or in the future.

CHAPTER IX.

FISH-PASSES.

So far, my remarks have been limited to the formation and improvement of fisheries in which it is proposed to cultivate

THE LAKE, FISH-PASS, AND DAM AT BATTLEBY.

non-migratory Salmonidæ—or, rather, what are generally known as non-migratory Salmonidæ. In the present chapter I propose to have something to say about opening out waters for the migratory fish, i.e., Salmo Salar, the salmon proper, and Salmo Trutta, the sea-trout. Of the value of these fish, both from a sporting and a marketable point of view, there can be no shadow of doubt, and their introduction into suitable waters is inevitably followed by an enormous increase in the value of the same. Yet, here again, we find hundreds of miles and thousands of acres of water which might contain them absolutely fishless so far as they are concerned.

It is quite obvious that an exhaustive discourse concerning the complex questions arising in connection with the cultivation of migratory Salmonidæ would be quite be-

THE ENTRANCE TO THE FISH-PASS AT BATTLEBY.

yond the scope of my present contribution to the literature of fish-culture; but a work on farming fish for pleasure and profit would, of necessity, be quite incomplete without some reference to the subject. I, therefore, propose to explain certain practical methods by means of which waters at present inaccessible to migratory fish may be populated by salmon and sea-trout. It may be that a fishery you have made, in accordance with plans I have explained, communicates with the sea by way of river or stream, but there exists some obstacle which prevents

H 2

fish running up from the sea to the fishery. These, then, are the matters with which I propose next to deal, and, in conjunction with a few hints given in the chapter on incubating and hatching fish-eggs, they comprise all I have to say on the subject at present.

The formation of lakes, the manipulation of river-beds, and the opening out of them to the sea, in order that salmon and sea-trout may mount to them in season, is a work of enormous importance, not only to individuals, but to the whole nation at large; so much so, indeed, that the process has been appreciated as an "opportunity" by the legal fraternity, and, in many cases, it is beset by legal objections, from which the fish-farmer has, at times, some difficulty in steering clear. Briefly, I may say that wherever any doubt occurs—and, for that matter, even where it does not occur to the non-legal mind—a few pounds spent in consulting a lawyer before any work of importance is undertaken is money well invested. You should also become acquainted with the "requirements" of the Board of Trade before erecting any fish-pass or other structure that is likely to influence any vested interest in a salmon fishery. Having done these things, you may be permitted to go ahead, and, if you are the fortunate owner of a length of river or a lake that may be made accessible to migratory Salmonidæ, your harvest will be a very rich one indeed.

I could particularise scores of cases in which very large sheets of water might be transformed into salmon and sea-trout lakes of great value, but I will refer here to two cases only, and these merely to point my argument. Lough Mask, in Co. Galway, Ireland, covers an area of over 25,000 acres, and this enormous lake could be made into a salmon and sea-trout loch and its tributary streams proportionately benefited if only a channel were cut and a fish-pass erected, so that Mask was in direct communication with the sea by way of Lough Corrib, and the work presents no engineering difficulties to speak of. In Argyllshire (Scotland) Loch Avich lies amidst charming surroundings, but a fall on the river Avich prevents it becoming a salmon and sea-trout loch. Yet, here again, this same fall presents very little, if any, difficulty to the pisci-cultural engineer; in other words, the erection of a fish-pass which would transform this beautiful sheet of water, four miles long by one mile wide, into a salmon loch would be quite a simple matter, and not an expensive one either. Astounding as these two cases are, they only go to form ex-amples of many others distributed over the whole of the British Isles, and when we consider, in addition, the miles and miles of river and stream that await treatment at the hands of modern practical piscicultural engineers, we better realise the immense possibilities associated with the encouragement of salmon and sea-trout into inland waters at present inacces-sible to them.

I am not forgetting that difficulties other than those of an engineering character occur; but they are surmountable also, even though they be of a legal nature. And, the difficulties being surmountable, it is more than strange to me that the possibilities are not turned to more practical account. Let us look at the matter in another light and let me suppose, for the purpose of illustration, that a certain sheep farmer has many thousand acres of admirable pasture land, and that it only requires to form a roadway to such pasture land in order to ensure the coming of a magnificent flock of sheep each year, and, comparatively speaking, free of expense. Need I ask whether or not the farmer would form the roadway, if at all possible? Yet, substitute salmon and trout for sheep, and, although the possibilities in this latter case are actually within reach, they are again and again, time out of number, absolutely neglected.

But such neglect does not always occur; and, in referring to what has been done and what is being done in connection with the opening out of water to migratory Salmonidæ, I shall en-deavour to show you how similar improvements could be made elsewhere. And let me also say at once that the work of planning and making a fish-pass or big dam is best carried out under the personal superintendence of an expert, and I know of no better man in this connection than Mr. P. D.

Malloch, of Perth, who has devised and superintended the
erection of the whole of the fish-passes with which I illustrate
this chapter, excepting that on the river Eden at Armathwaite.   The fact is that the erection of a fish-pass presents

THE FISH-PASS AT BATTLEBY, AS SEEN FROM ABOVE.

a different problem in nearly every situation, the solving of
which can only be accomplished by someone who has not only
a thorough knowledge of the habits of salmon and sea-trout,
but also an opportunity of thoroughly inspecting the condi-

tions under which such pass has to accomplish the object in view. I have inspected several so-called fish-passes, which have proved to be nothing more nor less than obstructions to running fish, and I have seen none that work so well or are so satisfactory in every way as those planned by Mr. Malloch. Some idea of his ingenuity in this direction may be gathered from the fact that he has just completed a scheme whereby salmon and sea-trout will be given access to what has seemed

TOP OF FISH-PASS AT DUPPLIN DYKE.

to be an impossible water hitherto. His scheme is actually an underground tunnel!

I think it will be best to give you some idea of what has been done in the formation of fish-passes before describing how the work has been accomplished, and I cannot do better in the first place than show and tell you something about the dam, lake, and fish-pass on the Schochie river, at Battleby, Perthshire.

A few years back the river Schochie (a tributary to the famous salmon river, the Tay) was an unpretentious stream, quite inaccessible to salmon and sea-trout. For a great part of its course it flows through the picturesque estate of Mr. Archibald Coates, and at Battleby a wonderful dam and fish-pass has been erected, with the result that there now exists a splendid lake well stocked with salmon and sea-trout in season, and with a magnificent head of rainbow trout, the latter grand fellows, running up to 7lb. or more in weight, and, big as they are, they rise freely to the fly and afford excellent

BOTTOM OF FISH-PASS AT DUPPLIN DYKE.

sport. All this, I repeat, has been brought about by the formation of the dam and fish-pass, of which I give some illustrations. The valley through which the Schochie river was wont to pursue its noisy course now lies buried beneath the bosom of a smiling lake of proud proportions. In addition, above the lake the river has been dammed back at different points, and in this manner some splendid fishing pools (about 20 in all) have replaced the tumbling stream of years ago. This is the result of the estate having fallen into the hands of an enthusiastic and skilful angler in the person of Mr. Coates, and it should be an object lesson to other owners of water who at present neglect to avail themselves of similar opportunities.

In connection with the lake and fish-pass at Battleby, it will be noticed that the prominent feature is the great dam; and it is evident that such a structure must be built by properly qualified workmen under the direction of an expert piscicultural engineer. Dams are necessary evils in fish-culture operations, and a few words concerning them may not be out of place just now, seeing that we have one of some importance before us. Livingston Stone never made a more weighty assertion than when he wrote: "If it is necessary to build a dam, I would recommend to the inexperienced to procure, by all means, the skill of an engineer or practical dam-builder who understands the nature of running water, for to confine running water securely is an art in itself, and a beginner is almost sure to make a mistake somewhere, for which in the end he will pay a heavy penalty in losses. . . . Employ an experienced man, then, to build the dam, if you must have one, and tell him to make it doubly safe; and even then, if your experience is like mine, you will be sorry you built it!" The dam at Battleby is built of massive proportions from solid concrete, and is of the form generally known as a "buttress" dam. It goes without saying that such work must be allowed to thoroughly "set" before any water is permitted to accumulate against it. But for ordinary purposes I have a liking for earth dams, and, most decidedly, in the case of small dams, they are much to be preferred, the precaution absolutely necessary in connection with them being to guard against the presence of rats or other animals that may undermine your work. Herr S. Jaffe, of Osnabruck, is a great believer, also, in earth dams, and I cannot do better than quote his advice in connection with this subject: "Before a dam is attempted, a good many things have to be calculated; before all, the maximum amount of storm water likely to gather after a sudden storm or cloud-burst, and a storm-water channel, with a very full allowance for this extra amount of flow has to be arranged for." (I explain this fully in the chapter on the formation of ponds

and lakes.) " The dam itself ought to be of earth only, and all
stones, rock, or rubble ought to be carefully picked out before
building the dam is commenced. Dams ought to be, across
their foot, even in very good holding soil (like clay and loam),

THE LUNCARTY FISH-PASS.

at least three times the width of the proposed depth of the
pond, and the crown of the dam ought to be, at least, half the
depth of the pond at its deepest part. Even this would apply
to comparatively shallow ponds only, say, of not over two

yards in depth at deepest part; and this would mean that, in the case of a pond two yards deep, the dam ought to be six yards, at least, across at foot and one yard at crown. . . . The weakest part of all ponds is the foot of the dam, and particularly at the foot of the outlet. The outlet upright "—(I have termed this outlet the controlling sluice in the chapter on screens and sluices)—" ought, therefore, to be at least two feet longer than the depth of the pond, and to be sunk below the level of the foot of the dam. The weak point at the foot of the dam may be overcome by removing (before beginning to build the dam) the turf over the whole width and length of the ground occupied by the dam, the turf to be laid back and afterwards to be used for covering the face of the dam. . . . Every barrowful of earth carted must be carefully and thoroughly stamped down. When the dam is finished water ought not to be turned on for three months, the dam to be allowed to settle and all damage by moles, rats, etc., to be made good before water is let in, which even then has to be done very gradually. It will be seen that making even a low retaining dam is not a job to be easily undertaken, and it will pay to call in at the outset professional help from a practical dam-builder." I quite endorse Herr Jaffe's opinions, and have nothing to add to them, only that, where possible, a dam built entirely from turfs, as I recommend in another chapter, is to be preferred even to plain earth; but the turfs should be cut with plenty of soil attached to them.

Before describing Mr. Malloch's designs for fish-passes, it is necessary that I should show you two others of his. These are the important pass on the river Earn (Perthshire), at Dupplin Dyke, and the Luncarty pass (Perthshire). In the former case an enormous number of salmon used annually to assemble in the water below the dyke, where it formed an impassable barrier. By-the-bye, this water is well known to at least some of my readers as the famous salmon and sea-trout fishery rented by Mr. Wynne Corrie, brother of Mr. E. Valentine Corrie, the fish-culturist of Winchester. By the erection of the pass many miles of additional water on the Earn are now populated by salmon and sea-trout in season, and, of course, the value of the fisheries so benefited has been considerably enhanced. A similar obstruction existed and has been overcome in the same manner at the point where the Luncarty pass has been erected. It will be noticed that in each case Mr. Malloch has adopted similar designs for the passes, and he was good enough to fully explain the working of his methods to me upon the occasion of my visits for the purpose of obtain-

A FISH-PASS, SHOWING ARRANGEMENT OF BOULDERS.

ing the photographs. And here again we find that the method owes its perfection to the simplicity and practical character of the design.

A properly designed fish-pass permits the fish to gain access to the waters above through a sufficient volume of water in the pass without being compelled to leave the water in the pass at any point or part for the purpose of leaping up and over any obstruction. Once understand this clearly, and the secret of success is yours. It does not follow that because a fish is seen leaping at a fall that it is sure to overcome the obstacle. It may do so, but it is equally possible that it may not. The perfect pass, then, is one through which the fish can run without the necessity of leaving the water at any part of it. Moreover, the water in the pass through which the fish swims must be "dark" water, i.e., it must not be foamy, "white" water. Hence it follows that a succession of falls with "white" water at the bottom of each do not go to form a perfect fish-pass, al-

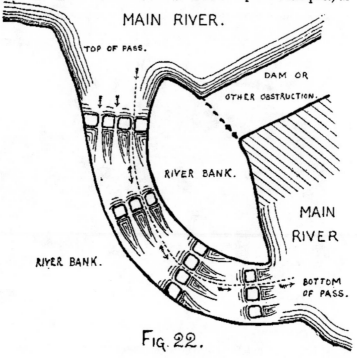

MAIN RIVER.

TOP OF PASS.

DAM OR

OTHER OBSTRUCTION.

RIVER BANK.

MAIN

RIVER

RIVER BANK.

BOTTOM OF PASS.

FIG. 22.

Fig. 22.—Plan of a Fish-pass.

though it is possible that a fish may mount up them by a succession of "leaps." The "step-by-step" principle is the one to be adopted in preference to any other; but the "steps" should be formed after the manner shown in the next illustration, and Fig. 22 explains how it is done. The drawing shows the position of the dam or other obstruction to be overcome, and it is also a plan of the fish-pass, with boulders so arranged that they are close enough to keep a sufficiency of water back and so form a succession of "step-by-step" pools, yet far

enough apart to permit of the fish passing from pool to pool in
a volume of water flowing between them (the boulders). The
dotted line and arrows show the direction of the current, and
also point to one of the many ways through the pass for the
fish. If necessary, they can rest at any part of the pass in the
slack water caused by the boulders, and this, in practice, they
are found to do when the pass is of considerable length. Needless to say, the fish mount against the arrows, entering, of
course, at the lower part of the pass. In the drawing the number of rows of boulders is less than would actually occur in a
pass, but sufficient to show the method of working. It is not
advisable to have more than a foot rise in each pool, and thus
an obstacle 10ft. high would be preferably overcome by a succession of 10 pools. In the same way, it is necessary to keep
the pools as long as possible, otherwise what is intended for a

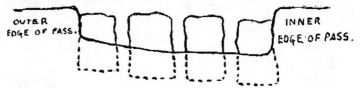

Fig. 23.—Section of a Fish-pass.

steady volume of " dark " water will become a broken, foam-
ing, " white " torrent, and no fish would attempt to run up it.
In Figure 23 you will see that the boulders are well let into
the bed of the pass and cemented firmly, otherwise they would
become washed out of place, and thus the whole scheme of the
pass would be destroyed.

In addition to the proper arrangement of the boulders in
the pass, two other matters of importance have to be taken
into serious consideration. The first of these is the fact that
the intake at the top of the pass must be wider than the pass
itself, or otherwise the latter would be short of water half
way down. The other point is that, in order to gain greater
length and consequently less abrupt " fall " in the pass, it is
preferably (although not absolutely necessary) constructed in
a curved or serpentine form, and this being so the volume of
water naturally flows in the direction of what I have termed

the outer edge of the pass in Fig. 23, and it would continue to "hug" that edge all through the pass, only that at the inner edge of the pass the depth is greater, as shown in the drawing, and the water is, therefore, encouraged to fall, as it were, towards the inner edge, and, in practice, this arrangement is found to effect a pretty equal flow of water throughout the entire length and over the whole extent of the pass.

This—the correct—principle of an efficient fish-pass has been applied in a very simple form to a weir on the Cumberland

FISH-PASS ON THE EDEN, AT ARMATHWAITE.

Eden, at Armathwaite. I give an illustration of this pass, and Fig. 24 explains the method of adapting the principle. The drawing shows the dam (or weir), and it will be noticed that a sufficient volume of "dark" water is collected and conducted over the obstruction at a certain point so as to enable the fish to run up through it. The desired result was obtained by bolting down large pieces of timber in such a position as to form a guide for and a means of collecting the volume of water necessary for the purpose. The water entering at the top of the pass is concentrated, and consequently increased in depth by the decrease of width between the timbers confining it lower down. The boulders shown—and several others—cause slack water and consequent resting places for the fish as they run through.

In concluding my remarks on fish-passes I would like to

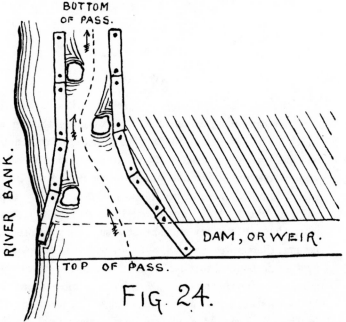

FIG. 24.

make it perfectly clear that, while I advocate the principle of so constructing a pass that the fish are enabled to run through the volume of water contained in the pass, I am quite prepared to admit that, under favouring circumstances, salmon " leaps " may be arranged for, with varying success, but they are not so successful as such a pass as I have described.

CHAPTER X.

SPAWNING.

In the cultivation of fisheries on scientific lines too much importance cannot be attached to the wisdom of the old adage which teaches that it is inadvisable to attempt to run before one has learned to walk. But the time comes to us all when we may venture to increase our knowledge; and the time will surely come to those of my readers who practically test the value of the hints I have given in the preceding chapters, when they will not remain content with merely forming fisheries and therein rearing fish, but they will wish to spawn their own stock fish and artificially hatch the ova so obtained; or, supposing they have no stock fish or an insufficient number of them to start with, they will be eager to proceed with the hatching of eggs obtained from some commercial fish-culture establishment.

In the case of spawners contained in a properly constructed pond such as I have described, it is a simple matter to catch the fish for the purpose of spawning. One draw of the net will be sufficient often for a morning's work in "stripping" and preparing the ova for the hatchery. It may be necessary to slightly lower the water in the pond, but this is not often the case, and it is inadvisable to do so unless it be absolutely necessary. Spawning operations should always be carried out in the early part of the day, so that time remains for securely "housing" the eggs before night. If you have to catch your spawners from waters in which they live a "wild" life, then you will have far more trouble. But the work of collecting

I

eggs from wild trout is considerably facilitated if the fish are caught from properly protected redds, such as I have already described. The work of obtaining salmon suitable for spawning purposes is still more difficult. "Collecting salmon eggs," wrote the late Sir James Maitland, "will remain a difficult business until fishery boards sufficiently understand the true interests of their districts and build proper ponds in which to retain the gravid fish until ripe." He goes on to mention how it took five days' netting at the mouths of the Almond and the Earn to obtain 175,000 salmon eggs, while, on the other hand, from his ponds at Howietoun, he obtained no less than 600,000 trout eggs himself in one morning! The enormous difference in cost is made clear from the fact that the expense of collecting salmon eggs ranges from ten shillings to fifteen shillings per thousand, which is more than treble the keep per annum of mature trout in stock-ponds per thousand eggs produced at spawning time.

Undoubtedly, the most valuable trout for spawning purposes are "wild" fish, and it follows that they are most easily and most economically netted from protected redds. If wild fish are not available or not obtainable of sufficient size, an alternative method of getting good spawners is to rear some fish—from known, and consequently suitable, parents—to the yearling stage (not beyond), turn them into waters at that stage, and allow them to run "wild" until they approach the completion of their fourth season, when they may be netted or caught out, transferred to proper stock-ponds or fenced-off lengths of river or stream, and thereafter kept in confinement and used for spawning purposes in due season. In some cases spawners reared in the latter manner are actually to be preferred to absolutely wild fish, especially when the wild fish are of small size. Artificially reared fish, and by this I mean fish which have been kept in confinement from the time of hatching, are not to be recommended for spawning purposes, but, nevertheless, they are, in some cases, not to be entirely condemned. It would appear that where such fish have the opportunity of getting a plentiful supply of natural food,

satisfactory results are obtained. It is where large quantities
of horse-flesh are used as food that absolute condemnation of
the fish for spawning purposes occurs. And for this reason :
A horse-flesh diet results in fatty degeneration of the ovaries.
There is no getting away from this fact. I shall have more to
say about the artificial feeding of trout presently ; meanwhile
I commend the foregoing remarks to the earnest consideration
of my readers, and would remind them that the same advice
holds good, of course, in connection with any eggs that may be
purchased.

It will be noticed that I have placed four years as the earliest age at which the eggs from a trout should be used for fish-
culture purposes. Some authorities go farther than this, and
affirm that old spawners are to be preferred, and by
old spawners are meant fish of from six to nine years
of age. The late Sir James Maitland wrote : " The
maturity of the parent fish is of paramount importance
in determining the chance of the offspring in the
struggle for existence. Old spawners produce strong
and healthy fry ; young spawners, though comparatively
more prolific, produce weaker offspring, with a much
smaller chance of holding their own in the waste of
waters." This is a most weighty and valuable statement ; but
in connection with it the fact must be taken into consideration
that the Howietoun Fishery is situated in a district where the
water is far lower in temperature for a greater part of the year
than it is in some of the waters in the South of England, and
consequently the fish, to which Sir James was more particularly indebted for his information, probably did not mature
quite so soon as do South-country fish. Be this as it may,
there is no doubt that spawners are more valuable at from five
to seven years of age, and that—with very few exceptions indeed—the fourth year is the first in which they are of any real
use to the fish-culturist who is desirous of doing good and
permanent work.

The operation of spawning a salmon or trout necessitates the
exercise of great care, even by an expert. From the com-

I 2

mencement of November onward, female trout begin to
" ripen," and when quite ready for spawning may be netted
from the river or stock-pond for that purpose.   Salmon, of
course, are obtained from the redds in their proper season also.
If there is a spawning house convenient to the ponds or river,
the operation of " stripping " the fish and impregnating the
ova is better carried out under cover, especially in rough weather; but unless the building is quite close it is advisable to
spawn out in the open and close by the water, if only for the
reason that the males will turn sulky should they be retained
from the water too long.   To spawn a salmon or trout, take
the fish firmly by the " wrist "—i.e., the fleshy part of the
body, between the vent and the tail—in the left hand, while
the right hand somewhat loosely encircles the head (or partly
encircles it, according to the size of the fish) at the gill covers.
The fish is then held so that its vent is directly over and
within about six inches of the spawning dish, which should be
quite dry and clean.   This article is in the form of a large
earthenware dinner-plate, but deeper, and it has a broad,
shallow lip added, which is most useful for the purpose of distributing the eggs over the bottoms of the hatching trays
later on.   These dishes are known in Scotland by the name of
milk-plates.   The operator now proceeds to " strip " the fish,
i.e., deprive it of the ova.   This process, in the case of trout of
less than 5lb. weight (which means a very large proportion of
trout handled) is performed by slightly bending back the fish,
which action causes the eggs to flow freely from the vent; or,
I ought rather to say, such action should cause the eggs to
flow.   If it does not, the fish is not " ripe," and it must be
returned to the water.   In the case of larger fish (salmon and
trout), the operator presses the fish's back against his breast
to obtain and retain more command over it.   Where fish of
very large size are stripped, it becomes necessary to have an
assistant, whose duty it is to control the tail or " wrist " parts
of the fish.   A fish will not always yield the whole of the eggs
it holds ; in a natural manner the time of spawning may extend over several days, the fish shedding some of their eggs

to-day and others to-morrow, and so on. Sometimes, therefore, a fish is handled that has been, in part, spawned before,
and only a few eggs remain to be released. These are obtained by very gently passing the right hand down the belly,
putting on very slight pressure when well past the vitals and
near the vent. Ova should never be forced from a fish in bulk,
but as many eggs as gentle treatment will permit of having
been obtained, the fish should be released and the operation of
stripping completed later on, when the remainder of the eggs
are ripe. It is a general rule, however, that the operation of
completely "stripping" a fish can be carried out at one and
the same time.

When the spawning-dish contains about ten thousand eggs,
a male fish is taken in hand, after a similar manner to the instructions in connection with "stripping" the female; then
a slight pressure just above and behind the pectoral fins has
the desired effect of causing the fish to emit a sufficient quantity of milt. It may happen—through sulkiness on the part
of the fish, or mis-handling on the part of the operator—that
the fish refuses to release its milt, and if this be the case it (the
fish) must be returned to the water, and one more tractable
taken in hand. Sir James Maitland was of the decided opinion
that if the abdomen of the male was held in contact with the
eggs a larger flow of milt was ensured. It is important to note
that the process of impregnation shall occur in the least possible space of time. As soon as the ova are impregnated, they
are thoroughly—but most carefully—stirred by the hand, in
order to ensure the milt reaching the largest possible number
of eggs. Then a small quantity of water is poured into the
dish, and thereafter the eggs must remain uninterfered with
until they separate. Be sure that the eggs have plenty of time
in which to separate; half an hour is not too long, or, in extreme cases, even an hour; but the former period of time
should be sufficient if the eggs have been thoroughly impregnated. When quite separated they are thoroughly washed in
clear water, and when this has been carefully done they are
taken to the hatchery, where they are placed in the hatching

trays for the purpose of incubation. The milt of one male
Fario is generally sufficient to impregnate 10,000 eggs of a
female of the same species ; but in the case of Irideus the milt
of one male fish should be used over not more than 5,000 eggs
One other point.   When spawning Irideus it will be found
that more moisture accompanies the eggs of the female fish
and this should be permitted, so that less water is necessary
in the spawning-dish after impregnation.

It is pretty generally accepted by all fish-culturists that the
periods at which the greatest loss occurs in connection with
the reproduction of the Salmonidæ in a natural manner are :
First, at spawning time, through imperfect impregnation
(only a proportion of the eggs becoming impregnated), and
through the ravages of the numerous enemies to fish eggs, including, of course, salmon and trout themselves ; and, second,
that period immediately succeeding the absorption of the umbilical sac.   The latter is dealt with in another place (see
rearing young fry), and the former is best remedied by artificially spawning the fish, as I have described above, and hatching them in a proper hatching house and in suitable trays,
after the manner I next propose to tell you.

CHAPTER XI.

HOW TO MAKE A HATCHERY.

The choice of a site for the hatching-house is dependent almost entirely upon the presence of a proper water supply.

A SETTLING BED.

It is possible to run the water some distance from the supply to the building, but it is not advisable to do so. The necessary condition, then, required in the choice of position may be stated in a few words as a continual supply of water that is pure and is of a low and even temperature throughout the incubating and hatching season. This condition is best realised if the hatchery is fed from a rock or ground spring, and should there be one on the estate that is the very best site for the hatching house ; and, having ascertained beyond any doubt that the spring is really pure and never failing, you may proceed to erect the building, or to properly equip any suitable structure that may already exist, without any further trouble, the water being merely conveyed to the hatchery direct.

Or you may obtain the supply of water from a stream or

PART OF A COMMERCIAL HATCHERY.

river of known purity ; but in this case it generally becomes advisable to pass the water through a settling bed before it enters the hatchery—even though filter beds may be erected in the hatchery—or otherwise trouble may arise from sediment in flood time. A good position to " tap " a stream is at a fall or cascade, or immediately below it, as at such a point the water is, of course, well charged with oxygen. In some fortunate cases the water supply may be drawn from a hillside stream of excellent quality water, and it only becomes necessary to conduct such water supply to the hatchery direct.

Failing any better supply, a mill-head or some embanked water may be tapped, passed through a settling bed, and so to the hatchery. But, whatever, the method of obtaining the necessary supply may be, this, let me repeat, is essential : A continual supply, which is pure and remains at a low temperature during the operations of incubation and hatching.

Settling beds should be of ample depth and size, and they are best constructed of brickwork sides and concrete bottom. This in order that they can be thoroughly cleaned from time to time, with least amount of trouble. Where any debris is brought down through the supply and into the settling bed, a lot of trouble may be avoided by placing some framed perforated zinc around the inlet, as shown in the illustration, which is from a photograph of a contrivance in use at Mr. Silk's fishery, at Wansford. If the water has to come from any distance it is best conveyed underground from the supply to the settling bed; and, in most cases, it becomes absolutely necessary to convey the supply from the settling bed underground to the hatchery. Glazed earthenware pipes are best for this purpose. The reason for conveying the water underground is to guard against stoppage of supply by the water becoming frozen, but it also prevents possible contamination. Constant attention must be given to the inlet of the settling bed, so that it does not become choked by debris or ice. The outlet from the settling bed should be well below the surface of the water, but not nearer to the bottom than about two feet. It should be of ample size, and should be protected by a slanting screen—a pair of screens, one of much finer perforation than the other is better—and a sluice should be added in order to control the bulk of water supplied to the hatchery. The exact amount of water run over the eggs is arranged for in a manner to be described presently.

Whether you convert an existing building to the purpose or erect one especially, as with the water supply, so with the building; it is of great importance to guard against frost. In other words, the water supply inside the hatchery should never reach freezing point. To avoid this is not so difficult

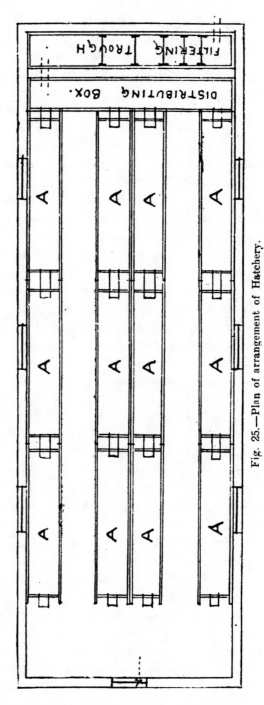

Fig. 25.—Plan of arrangement of Hatchery.

a matter as it might at first appear to be. Various materials, or combinations of materials, of a more or less expensive nature, have from time to time been recommended and used; but the simplest, and best to my way of thinking, is what is known as a thatched building. Really practical farmers are quite aware of the great value of thatched barns and buildings; in them can be stored any description of root or cereal crop—or animals may be housed in them—without the slightest fear of frost; while the comfort (from a climatic point of view) of thatched dwelling-houses can only be properly appreciated by those who have lived in them. In the thatched building, then, the fish-culturist finds the most suitable structure for the purpose of a hatching house; and, as well as being the best, it is one of the most economical. Moreover, if a little taste be exercised in design, it can be made quite picturesque. The walls should be of brickwork, but frameworks should fit them on the outside, and these frameworks should be thatched; framework shutters (also thatched) should be made to fit the windows and doorways. These thatched frameworks need not necessarily be used only when a severe frost is imminent, but they should be available in case they are wanted. If the building is in a very exposed position, it may be lined inside with common felt, in addition to the thatch outside, but the felt is seldom necessary. For my own part, I prefer to see the plain brickwork inside; and bricks with a glazed surface are best; they look nice, are easily cleaned, and cost very little more money. The windows should be fitted with green blinds—or curtains—to subdue the light.

The floor should be of concrete, cemented over and made to fall in the direction of one or more channels (according to the size of the building), cut with the object of carrying off the water that is sure to be spilt in course of the operations. Stout frameworks should be erected on which the hatching boxes are to be placed, and these I describe presently, but I may say here that the "stands" or framework on which the boxes rest must be of a thoroughly substantial character, as it is of importance that the hatching boxes should remain perfectly steady during the period the eggs are being incubated.

As I have alredy remarked, if the water supply is obtained direct from a spring, it may be conducted direct to the hatchery, into the distributing box or boxes, and thence into the hatching boxes and over the eggs. The distributing box is made on exactly the same principle as one of the distributing ponds shown in Fig. 10 in the chapter on the formation of lakes and ponds; only, of course, the distributing box in the hatchery is but a pond in miniature. The object, however, is the same, i.e., to control and evenly distribute the water supp'y to each set of hatching boxes independently. If the water supply requires to be filtered, then the filter is placed at the head of the hatching house, and the water passes through it before reaching the distributing box. Any effective filter may be used, but the simplest and best I know of for the purpose is formed by placing a number (more or less, according to the requirements of the case) of flannel screens across a long wood trough. The inlet is at one end of the trough, the outlet at the other; consequently, the water has to pass through the flannel screens before leaving the filtering trough. A number of spare flannel screens are provided, so that, as one lot is removed for cleansing purposes, others can be slid in. The general appearance of a properly equipped hatchery is shown in the next illustration; and Figs. 25 and 26 explain the relative position of the filtering trough, distributing box, and hatching boxes. Of course, the size of the hatchery depends entirely upon the extent of the operations, and the room required for a certain number of eggs is referred to in the remarks that follow. Just a few words of advice in this connection : Do not cramp yourself for room, or you will live to curse the day you ever did so. One requires plenty of " elbow room " when engaged upon the important work connected with the incubation and hatching of fish-eggs.

In Figs. 25 and 26 the hatching boxes are marked A; in Fig. 26 the distributing box is marked B, and the filtering trough C.

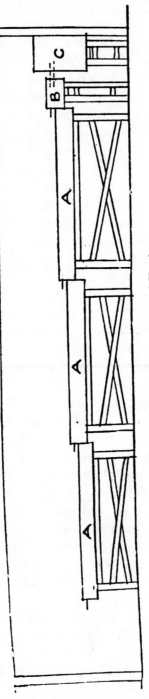

Fig. 26.—Section of arrangement of Hatchery.

Having obtained a suitable building, the next matter is to equip it after a proper manner. The first consideration is the method of making the stands on which are placed the filter, the distributing box, and the hatching boxes. As I have already pointed out, these should be of a thoroughly substantial character, and of all forms of stand I much prefer those made of strongly-framed, well-seasoned wood. Err, if at all, on the side of strength, for nothing is more likely to cause trouble than shakily contrived stands. Each season these stands should be carefully overhauled, cleansed, and varnished —as, indeed, the whole of the apparatus used should be. If the extent of hatching boxes is such as to occasion the lower boxes to be too near the floor of the hatchery, then such

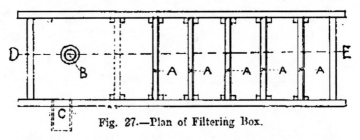

Fig. 27.—Plan of Filtering Box.

floor should be made to fall at the same gradient as that formed by the boxes. From 3ft. to 3ft. 6in. is a convenient distance from the floor at which the top of the hatching boxes should be.

The first important item of apparatus is the filtering box, and the principal matter in connection with its construction is to make sure that its capacity is amply sufficient to cope with any call that may be made upon it. Its actual size is determined by the amount of water required for hatching purposes, and its capacity should be such as to provide an output of quite half as much again water in addition to the actual quantity required. If the quantity of water required is very great, then two, or more, filtering boxes of moderate size are to be preferred to one of very large size. Of course, if the water supply is obtained from a spring, or other source that needs no filtration, a filtering box is unnecessary; but, should one be needed, then proceed to make it after the following manner:—

Form the box of strong wood planks, carefully tongued, grooved, bolted, and screwed together, and well char and varnish it inside after making. Fig. 27 is a plan of such a box, and Fig. 28 is a section of the same through a line D E of Fig. 27. The water supply enters the hatchery, and is conducted to the filtering box by an independent pipe. It is permitted to fall into the box at the upper part, marked F F, in Fig. 28. It passes through the flannel screens, marked A, in the direction shown by the arrows, and flows into the distributing box by way of the outlet, the position of which is marked at c. This outlet is placed in such a position that it

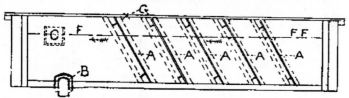

Fig. 28.—Longitudinal Section of Filtering Box.

ensures the water being kept at an average height shown by the line F F F, in Fig. 28. At B is provided a plug-hole and plug; this for the purpose of emptying the filter for cleansing purposes. Such operation should not be often necessary, and it will not be if the screens are carefully looked to, as these latter naturally collect most of the sediment. The box is provided with a lid, marked G, which should be kept in position at all times other than those during which the screens require attention. This lid has an aperture cut in it at the upper end to permit of the water flowing—or, rather, falling—into the box when the lid is on. A similar aperture occurs in the case of the lids to the distributing box, and also the hatching boxes. It requires to be of sufficient size to guard against any of the water splashing on the lid and so to the floor, being thus lost so far as supply is concerned, beside causing an unnecessary mess. The screens are formed from wood frames, on which is stretched some coarse flannel. They are placed in position, slanting away at the top in the direction of the current, for reasons already explained in slanting screens for ponds, etc. They are kept in position by means of slats screwed on the sides of the boxes, two of which go to form a groove down which the screen is slidden. These screens and the method of keeping them in the proper position are better explained in the next drawings. In Figs. 27 and 28 I show five screens, but the actual number necessary is determined by the quantity of sediment in the water when it reaches the hatchery. The flannel on the screens may, advisably, vary in coarseness, those nearest the outlet being, of course, the finest. If very much sediment comes into the box

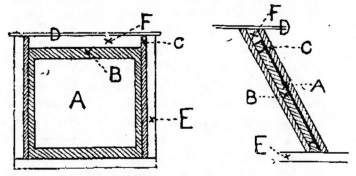

Fig 29.—Cross Section of Filtering Box.

Fig. 30.—Section of Screen.

in the first place it is advisable to let the screens terminate some two or three inches from the top of the box. In this way, should one of the screens clog during the absence of the attendant, the water will flow over the top of it, and so on to the next. If this precaution be not taken, the result may be of a disastrous nature, for the water, instead of flowing through the screens and so into the distributing box, may overflow in the first section between the first screen and the inlet end of the box, and leave the outlet section so low that not a sufficient supply will flow through the outlet and so into the distributing boxes. This means no flow of water through the hatching boxes, which in its turn spells death to your trout in embryo—if it continues any appreciable length or time. The prevention of such disaster is a simple matter, all that is required being proper attention to the screens. But I may well emphasise the importance of keeping the screens below the surface of the box, and I show them in this position in the next drawings. Fig. 29 is a section across the filtering box at one of the screens, and Fig. 30 is a section showing the method of fixing the slats at the back and front of the screen so that they form a groove on each side of the box. A is the flannel screen, B is the framework of the screen, C is the slat, D is the lid of the box, E is the framework of the box, and F is the space left for the water to flow over the screens in case of any of them becoming clogged with sediment. It should be noticed that the bottom of the frame of the screen is bevelled, so that it fits snug and accurately to the bottom of the box. Screens fixed in this manner are never any cause of trouble by floating. They may be quite easily cleaned by allowing them to get dry, when the sediment can be lightly brushed or dusted off. For this reason, and for others which I have previously explained, a few spare screens are very useful; indeed, they are necessary. If the water is very full of sediment of a somewhat coarse nature, the first and second screens may be of fine wire gauze, but, as a rule, the flannel will be found to be all that is necessary. The screen next the outlet should be removed as seldom as possible, and even then a duplicate should be ready to put into position immediately. This screen should always remain in position while the water in the filtering box is being lowered by means of the plug-hole, but the other screens should be removed, and, of course, the main supply shut off. One other caution: Let the plug-hole be amply big, so that the process of lowering the water in the box is rapidly effected.

Fig. 31 shows a useful form of outlet spout for the supply to the filtering box, for the filtering box, and for the distributing box; and Fig. 32 is a plan of the spout. It is fitted with a small hand sluice, of which there must be a number, with different size holes at C to regulate the quantity of water

h

flowing through.   The same form of spout, only without the
hand sluice, is used for the hatching boxes also.   In the
drawings A is the spout, B the sluice, C the hole to regulate
the supply, and D the front or side of the box.

The distributing box is quite a plain affair, and its position
(at right angles) in relation to the hatching boxes is shown in
Fig. 25.   It is fitted with a spout (Fig. 31) at the head of
each range of hatching boxes, to enable the supply to such
boxes being adjusted independently of the others.   It needs
no further explanation.

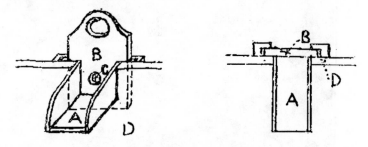

Fig. 31.—Outlet Spout and Hand Sluice.

Fig. 32.—Plan of Outlet Spout and Hand Sluice.

The next illustrations are of a hatching box and a hatching
tray—or basket, as it is sometimes termed.   I recommend
these trays and boxes in preference to any others; they are
simple, practical, economical, and strong.   Fig. 33 is a plan
of the box showing the arrangement of the trays.   A convenient size for the box (inside measurement) is 6ft. long by
15in. wide by 8in. deep.   It should be made of inch planking
and charred and varnished inside.   The hatching trays are
marked A, the outlet spout B, and C is a slanting board that
receives the supply of water and directs it under the trays.

Fig. 34 is a longitudinal section of the hatching box.   It
will be noticed that the slanting board C is kept at about 1½in.
from the bottom of the box, this to enable the water to flow
under it in the direction shown by the curved arrow; it is
kept in this position by a small stop fastened on the slats
which support it.   The trays, marked A, are kept at a conve-

nient distance from the bottom of the box by small iron supports fastened in the sides of the trays, as presently explained. These are marked b in the drawing. The handles to the trays are shown in section at a. The level of water in the box is shown by the dotted line F E. Some importance must be attached to the height at which the water is maintained in the hatching box during the process of incubation. Supposing the depth of the box to be 8in., then the top of the trays should be ⅜in. from the top of the box, the depth of the trays

A HATCHING BOX.

should be 4in., and the bottom of the trays should be 3in. clear from the bottom of the box. This leaves ¼in. for "play," and for the thickness of the sheet of perforated zinc which forms the bottom of the trays. The spout B should be so arranged that the water level in the box is 5in. above the bottom of the box. This permits of 3in. depth of water under the bottom of the trays, and 2in. of water flowing over the eggs in the trays. The correct volume of water necessary to flow through the boxes is referred to in my remarks on incubation. Each hatching box should be fitted with an outlet plug-hole and plug, shown at G in Fig. 34; this to enable each box to be emptied and cleaned or otherwise dealt with inde-

pendently of the others.   This plug should be of not less than
1in. diameter, and 1¼in. is a safer size.   The direction of the
current is shown by the arrows.   A long slat floated between
the two rows of trays will keep them in better "line," and is

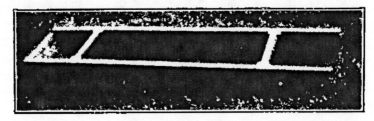

A HATCHING TRAY.

advisably added.   The boxes should be fitted with wood
covers, which should always be in position during incubation,
excepting, of course, when the eggs are being looked over and
attended to.

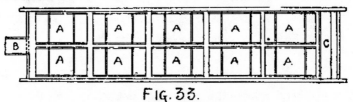

FIG. 33.

Fig 33.—Plan of Hatching Box.

The hatching trays are far and away the simplest and best
I know of.   They are made of two wooden "boat-shaped"
sides, and to the curved edges of these is fastened a strip of
perforated zinc.   The trays are similar in shape to a "swing-

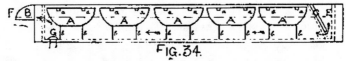

FIG. 34.

Fig. 34.—Longitudinal Section of Hatching Box.

boat."   In Fig. 35 I have imagined that one can see through
the front side of the tray.   A is the wooden side ; B B B the
strip of perforated zinc, which forms the bottom and ends
of the tray all in one ; c c are handles fitted across the top of

the tray, by means of which the trays can be easily handled, and, moreover, they materially assist in stiffening the tray. It will at once be seen that this shape of tray combines, in a wonderfully simple manner, all the best qualities essential. It presents a slanting surface to the flow of water, and there are no corners for the alevins (later on) to get jammed into. The sides may be made of perforated zinc also, but this is not necessary, and, moreover, the wood sides enable the tray to be "floated" in the washing box, when the egg shells are being cleared out at hatching time, or on other occasions when it is necessary to make use of the washing box. Fig. 36

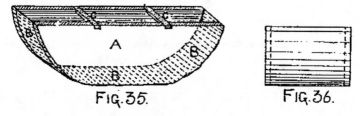

FIG. 35.   FIG. 36.

Fig. 35.—A Hatching Tray.

Fig. 36.—End View of a Hatching Tray.

is an end view of the tray. I do not recommend these trays being made of a large size, but a box of the dimensions already given may be made to hold eight only, instead of ten, as shown in the drawings.

This design of tray originated with the German pisciculturists. The photos. I give were taken at the Earl of Denbigh's hatchery at Holywell, North Wales.

The hatchery is now fitted, with the exception of a washing box, which is a most useful adjunct. An empty hatching box may be used for the purpose; but, should all the hatching room be required, then a plain box with a big plug and outlet should be fitted up in some convenient part of the hatchery. If specially made, this washing box should be deeper than an ordinary hatching box; 1ft. is not too deep.

Having ascertained that everything connected with the water supply and the apparatus I have just described is in perfect working order, and that the latter is scrupulously clean, you may proceed with the work of incubation; and I will pick up the thread of my discourse where the fish had been spawned, the eggs allowed to separate, and all is in readiness for placing them in the hatching trays.

CHAPTER XII.

INCUBATION AND HATCHING.

The incubation of fish-eggs calls for constant care and attention on the part of the fish-culturist. To the novice the season of incubation is a time of wondering expectation; to the expert it has been for all time, and remains, the most fascinating and one of the most critical stages of his year's work. Yet, if constant care and attention be exercised, the process is simple, and the consequent results of a most satisfactory nature.

The first thing to be done is to transfer the ova from the vessel in which it has been thoroughly rinsed—after separation has taken place—to the hatching trays, and this is done in the following manner: Ascertain that the temperature of the water in the vessel containing the ova is similar to that in the hatching boxes. If there should be any difference, adjust it by allowing the water from the hatching box to slowly flow into the vessel until any difference in temperature no longer exists. The water is drawn from the hatching box for this purpose most conveniently by means of a syphon formed by a length of ordinary ¾in. indiarubber tubing. You will find plenty of other use for this rubber syphon, and others of various sizes, as the work proceeds; therefore, have a few at hand, and make sure they are perfectly clean before attempting to use them at any time. When the temperature of the water in the hatching box is the same as that in the vessel containing the ova the eggs may be transferred to the box after the following manner: Adjust the water in the box so that it is at its normal height, then shut off the supply. Now take the vessel and carefully "float" out a sufficient number of eggs to fairly cover the surface of perforated zinc in one of the trays. Do not crowd the eggs. If they do not float out evenly and some lie on top of the others, alter this by very gently rocking the tray while the eggs still remain under water; or they may be "stroked" into proper position with the help of a feather.

Your next care is to adjust the supply of water flowing over the eggs; and in this connection I cannot do better than take as a basis the water supply at Howietoun, as, without doubt,

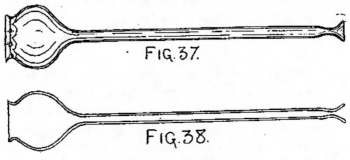

Fig. 37.—An Egg Extractor.
Fig. 38.—Section of Egg Extractor.

at that establishment is the best hatchery in the kingdom. There are five boxes in a line; each box holds about 16,000 eggs; thus each series of five boxes contains, say, 80,000 eggs. That number is the maximum. Over these is run not less than 2 gallons of water per minute in the early stages of incubation, increasing to $2\frac{1}{2}$ gallons per minute towards hatching time, and at actual hatching time as much as three gallons per minute may be run over them with beneficial results. This quantity of water is sufficient to command satisfactory incubation of 80,000 eggs. But if only one box holds eggs, the same quantity should be run over the 16,000 (or even a lesser number) as over the 80,000. Keep a constant and careful eye on the water supply, and remember that from the time of spawning every step towards hatching has a marked effect for good or evil on the future welfare of the young fish.

Your next care is to remove all white eggs. If the eggs
have been thoroughly impregnated at spawning these should
be few, but there are sure to be some. This advice holds good
right up to the time of hatching; indeed, most probably, a
few white eggs will remain over even after hatching is completed. It is almost needless for me to explain that the white
eggs are dead. In removing them be very careful, more especially in the early stages of incubation, not to disturb the surrounding fertile eggs. Be sure to remove all white eggs as
soon as they are seen; neglect of this precaution may result
in a disastrous attack of byssus—commonly called fungus.
As a matter of fact, the eggs should be carefully gone over
every day and all white ones removed. Keep the hatching
boxes covered with the lids at all times when not engaged
upon looking over the eggs.

Various forms of "egg extractors" have been devised for
the purpose of removing the white eggs, but I know of no
more simple or perfect instrument than that used at Howietoun. This I illustrate in Figs. 37 and 38. Any glass-blower
will make you a few of them. They are formed from a length
of $\frac{1}{4}$in. (inside measurement) glass tubing, with a swelled and
"necked" bulk at one end and a constriction formed at the
other. The shape is clearly shown in Fig. 38. Over the bulb
end is stretched a piece of indiarubber, and the instrument
then has the appearance as shown in Fig. 37. As explained
by Sir James Maitland, pieces of old tobacco pouches make excellent covers for these egg-extractors. They are used in the
following manner: The thumb is gently pressed on the indiarubber; this forms a vacuum in the bulb. Next the extractor is advanced in the water (still retaining pressure on the
indiarubber) until the constricted end is immediately over the
egg to be extracted. By removing the pressure of the thumb
on the indiarubber the egg is sucked up and held tight in the
constricted end, and is prevented travelling right up the tube
by the constriction. If this constriction did not exist there
would arise the necessity of removing the indiarubber before
the egg could be released from the tube. But with the con-

striction all that has to be done is to lift the egg out of the water and then press the indiarubber with the thumb, as before, when the egg is immediately released and falls from the tube. In practice the process is most simple.

Another very useful little article in the hatchery is illustrated by Figs. 39 and 40. A plain glass tube, ⅜in. inside measurement, is slightly bent, as shown in Fig. 39. When used as a syphon it is very handy for examining alevins, more especially in their advanced stages, as it permits of them being contained in the bend of the tube and in a quantity of water sufficient to allow them to swim and dart about. The

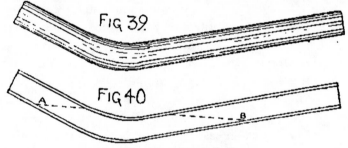

Fig. 39.—Glass Hand Syphon.

Fig. 40.—Section of Hand Syphon.

level of the water contained in the tube is shown by the dotted line A B in Fig. 40.

Be careful, and guard against sediment. A very slight amount of this—which may be carefully washed off by a gentle depression, or raising, or rocking of the tray—is not of vital importance; but it is best absent altogether, therefore, if the slightest sign of it is discovered, remedy the evil at once in the settling tank or in the filter. When the eggs are further advanced towards hatching, and may be thoroughly washed (preferably by means of an ordinary garden watering can) without harm resulting, sediment is an item of smaller importance; but even then it is better absent. Guard against shaking the eggs from twenty-four hours after laying them down till they are eyed. I have previously explained that the period of incubation varies with the temperature of the water; but, in a suitable temperature, which should be about forty-five degrees, the time occupied will be about eighty days. It is stated on good authority that salmon ova have been known to hatch in thirty days, and that they have taken as long as one hundred and forty days.

If perfect cleanliness is observed, a copious and pure supply of water maintained, care taken to thoroughly impregnate the eggs, and perfect quiet in the hatchery strictly enforced, the work of incubation should proceed in a perfectly satisfactory manner. It is want of, or temporary neglect of, these necessary precautions that causes trouble, and, trouble having once originated in connection with the operations, it may very easily prove disastrous. Fungus, for instance, is quite easily prevented; but it is most difficult to eradicate where it is permitted to occur. Even where it is " cured," the eggs or young fish once attacked by it are never so strong again.

After a little experience, you will be able at various stages to calculate the chances of complete success at hatching time, and to distinguish between the fairly good and the very good eggs, and to conduct your operations in accordance with such discovery. About half-way through incubation is the first stage of the eggs becoming eyed, and they may now stand very careful handling for the purpose of examination. All the unfertilised eggs will also be quite easily distinguished at this stage. When the eggs are " fully eyed " is the time to transplant them to redds outside, after the manner I have already described. In this way the stock of eggs in the hatching boxes may be reduced one-half with advantage.

When hatching commences, fermentation will occur, and removal of the shells demands attention; and now the advantages of having at least one box in each row empty, or the addition to the hatchery of a " washing " box, becomes apparent. First the quantity of water flowing through the boxes has to be increased, as I have already advised; second, the shells must be removed as soon as possible. The increased flow of water will counteract fermentation; but, in addition, the trays containing the alevins—i.e., the newly-hatched fish—may be taken to the washing box, or spare empty hatching box, and therein the alevins can be thoroughly but gently washed, and all egg-shells removed. This latter is simply done by first raising the tray in the water until the zinc bottom is only just covered with water; then quickly, but gently, depress the tray. The alevins will remain, for the most part, on the bottom of the tray; the eggs will float, or a large proportion of them will do so, on or near the surface, and they can be skimmed off. In this manner the greater bulk can be removed; but a few shells are sure to remain, and these may be removed by means of the hand-syphon shown in figs. 39 and 40. Every little bit of shell must be removed. Now is the time, also, to carefully examine the alevins and remove all weaklings, twins, and other monstrosities: these latter being perfectly useless, and only occupying room valuable for the other fish. Before the trays containing the alevins are placed back in the box, the latter should be thoroughly cleansed, and from the time of hatching until the alevins or fry are transferred outside to ponds, let constant care and attention be given to maintaining perfect cleanliness in the boxes. At the actual time of hatching, as many of the shells should be cleaned out as is possible before the trays are removed for the complete clearance of shells in the washing box. Sometimes it will happen that the eggs in a few trays in different boxes will hatch before the bulk contained in a box. When this is the case, a full box of alevins may be made up from trays obtained from several boxes. Note that the first box to be filled with alevins in trays is the one at the head of the row; this in order to guard against any bits of shell being brought down from boxes in which hatching is taking place above.

I have said that if attention is paid to the actual requirements of the hatchery no fear need be entertained of an attack of fungus. This is so. Any neglect will result in the white eggs being attacked by Byssus (Septomitris clavatus), and the consequent suffocation of the surrounding fertile eggs; for, although Byssus only attacks dead eggs, its growth from them in all directions is very rapid, and surrounding eggs are soon covered. Therefore, I repeat, remove all white eggs at once, and no trouble will arise. But there is a worse danger than an attack of Byssus to be feared, if constant care is not exercised; this is an attack of fungus proper, Saprolegnia, which spells disaster wherever it occurs. As prevention of even this is possible, on no account neglect the precaution. I must also impress upon all the vast importance of subdued light only being admitted to the hatchery.

Having advanced the eggs to the hatching stage, our next consideration is the care of the alevins and young fry.

CHAPTER XIII.

CARE OF ALEVINS AND YOUNG FRY.

The alevins may be left in the trays until hatching is quite completed; the use of the trays may then be dispensed with, the alevins being tipped into the box itself and the trays thoroughly cleansed, dried, and varnished, and put away for another season. But, before the fish are transferred from the trays to the boxes, the equipment of the latter has to be looked to, and this is the next matter for consideration.

In Fig. 34 it will be noticed that the slanting board c is used while incubation is going forward. First remove this board so that the water falls into the box direct from the spout of the box above. Next have ready a screen, which is to be placed in position at the lower end of the box; it should slant, as should all other similar screens used in fish-culture, at a decided angle, and should be covered with No. 9 perforated zinc. Be careful about the size of the perforation. With No. 9 you are quite safe, for if the alevins are forced against the screen, and any of their delicate umbilical sacs are drawn into a smaller perforation than No. 9, the alevin will be unable to extricate itself from its disagreeable position, and will most surely die. The screen should slant from the bottom to the top in the direction of the current, i.e., towards the outlet spout. The bottom of the screen should be in such a position as to leave the outlet plug G quite clear : about one foot from the end of the box is a convenient distance. The screen must fit absolutely accurately to the sides and bottom of the box; the slightest crevice will prove a

simple means of suicide on the part of the alevins, and one of
which they will not fail to avail themselves. The general
method adopted to make a perfect fit of the screen (and I
know of no better) is to make it so that it slides quite freely
into position, then fasten a strip of new, coarse flannel along
the two ends and the bottom, and, when this is done, gently
drive the screen into position, and it will be found to be
perfectly tight. The flannel should be new, as it fits much
closer. When the screen is in position, and the box is
cleaned, you may empty the alevins from the trays into the
box. Be gentle, and "float out" as many as possible; should
a few stubborn ones still remain in the tray, they may be
very carefully washed out by submerging the tray and rocking it from side to side. Do not forget that the little fish
are quite easily injured at this delicate stage of growth.

If, as I pointed out in the previous chapter, perfect cleanliness is observed in the boxes, there should occur only a very,
very small percentage of loss among the alevins until they
reach the stage at which they start to feed, and this occurs,
with healthy fish, a few days before the complete absorption
of the umbilical sac. Indeed, the alevins require little care
other than this important item of cleanliness. It will be
found that the little fish "pack" in masses; this is a good
sign, and it should occur when they are in the trays, and
also for some two or three weeks after they have been
transferred from the trays to the box. As the alevins gain
strength, a bigger volume of water may be sent through the
boxes, the quantity being gradually increased throughout,
say, one month, until the total amount flowing through
reaches from four to four and a half gallons per minute,
according to the size of the boxes, a four-gallon supply being
about right for the size of box I have described. It will be
found that the alevins actually scour the bottom of the box;
but some sediment will accumulate between the screen and
the outlet of the box, and this sediment should, without fail,
be removed each morning by means of one of the rubber
syphons. The sides of the box should be carefully watched,

and any accumulation of dirt of the slightest character immediately removed by means of a hand brush; after each brushing it should be ascertained that any dirt so removed is carried away by the current. The screen should be constantly brushed, especially on the under side, care being taken, of course, not to injure any alevins that may be driven on to, or be resting on, the upper surface of the screen. The bottom and sides of that portion of the box between the screen and the outlet should also be thoroughly brushed, at least, once a week; this in addition to the daily syphoning. The alevins can stand more light than the eggs, but even they must have but little. I have found that frames covered with common blue " veiling " form excellent tops to boxes containing alevins; they exclude light and admit more air than do wooden lids.

After a time the alevins will not " pack " so much, and a number of them will be found to dart and swim about the whole length of the box, frequently rising to and breaking the surface of the water. Then they will head up stream, and the strongest of them will be found swimming against the strong current at the head of the box—some of them right under the fall of water from the box above. They are " coming on the feed "; and now has arrived another most important stage of fish-culture. Indeed, many fish-culturists consider this to be the most critical stage of all.

CHAPTER XIV.

SOME ADDITIONAL REMARKS CONCERNING REARING FRY AND YEARLINGS.

In previous chapters I have had occasion again and again to refer to the possibilities of rearing fry on natural and artificial redds and in specially-made fry ponds; but there is no doubt that where inside rearing boxes are available they are very useful for the purpose of teaching young fish to feed. I am not forgetting that some fish-culturists transfer fry to outside waters as soon as they commence to feed; but I am convinced that they can be carried forward a stage further in rearing boxes under complete control with advantageous results. And this opinion in no way qualifies the statements I have made concerning the value of properly protected redds and properly formed fry ponds. Inside rearing boxes merely go to form another link in the chain of apparatus by means of which fish-culture may be pursued with some certainty of success. One of the principal items in connection with rearing fish is to gradually introduce them to deeper and deeper water of more and more volume until the maximum depth and volume is reached. To transfer a quantity of alevins direct from the boxes in which they have been hatched to deep outside ponds or to strong rivers of heavy volume is to court disaster. This is why I have, right throughout my discourse, insisted upon the necessity of having all fish-farming redds and ponds under control, so that fish may be gradually introduced into the depth and volume of water in which they are intended to provide sport. This is why I have emphasised the use of sluice boards, by

L

means of which the depth of water in the fry ponds may be increased as the fish advance in age and size. And this is why I consider inside rearing boxes to be a valuable link in the chain of apparatus. The depth of water in the boxes may be gradually increased by placing strips of flannel across the outlet spout. When the greatest possible depth has been attained in the boxes, the depth of water into which the fish are placed outside should only be a slight increase at first on that of the water in the boxes; this, in its turn, is increased, and so on. And it will be remembered that the shape of the bottom of the ponds which I recommend permits of the fish gradually frequenting deeper water of their own accord. Do not think that I place too much importance on this gradual increase in depth and volume of water. It is one of the greatest secrets of success. And my present advice will be found to coincide with that given in connection with the management of redds, and permitting the fish to gradually drop down from them into deeper water.

The importance of strictly attending to the advice tendered above becomes very evident when the matter of feeding is taken into consideration. If a number of alevins or young fry are plumped into deep water, nine-tenths of them will spread out upon the bottom and literally starve themselves to death's point. No amount of coaxing will induce them to herd together and feed freely, as they should do. But they can be taught to feed in shallow water, and then will continue to do so in water that is gradually increased in depth and volume.

You may start, then, to teach fry to feed in the rearing boxes, and as soon as they come well on the feed they should be transferred to water in the open. This should be not more than a fortnight after they first start to take food. Be very careful at the time of transfer that the temperature of the water into which the fish are put is exactly the same as that from which they are taken, and, should this entail much adjustment, let the work be done very gradually. Sudden change of temperature—however slight—spells disaster. As soon as the fish are outside, everything depends upon success in teaching them to look for their food, and take it, freely; and this important end can only be attained by constant care and careful watching. At the start, feed often, feed regularly, and never give too much food at a time. See also that, as far as possible, every fish gets its share of food. When possible, only one, and always the same attendant should feed the very young fish. If your operations are on such a scale as to demand the services of more than one attendant, then let each have charge of a particular number of fish, and feed those, and those only. Beyond doubt, the fish get to know their attendant, and will feed in his presence, while, perhaps, refusing to do so in the presence of a stranger. Remember, the absolutely imperative condition of success in this stage is to coax your fish to take food freely; but do not give them too much at a time, or trouble will result in that direction. If your ponds have been properly handled, and well stocked with natural food, your task will be lessened; but, under the most favourable circumstances, artificial food is an absolute necessity where anything like a large number of fish are to be reared; and this brings us to the next important consideration, i.e., the best artificial food to use.

In previous chapters I have emphatically stated my objections to a horse-flesh diet, and have given reasons for those objections. I plump in favour of fish-meal for yearlings, and Burgess' "Challenge" fish-food for fry. My choice of the latter for fry is arrived at simply because it contains a certain useful percentage of properly prepared meat, and my reason for nominating fish-meal as the best artificial food for yearlings and bigger fish is that, although it does not grow such abnormally big fish, it produces healthy stock, and, in combination with plenty of natural food, forms a perfect and all-necessary diet for trout. I venture to assert that horse-flesh for fish in confinement is quite an exploded idea, and I firmly believe that it has done more to produce non-rising and consequently non-sporting fish than many

L 2

people realise.   And, after all, it must not be forgotten that
fish-farming in the British Isles should be, is, and will continue to be, principally conducted with a view to an increase
of sport rather than an increase of food supply, although I
do not dream of ignoring the importance of its bearing upon
the latter.   Moreover, there is no doubt that trout fed on
horse-flesh never develop such beautiful markings and correct
contour of form as do those fed on meal.   Then, again, there
is the difficulty of getting horse-flesh fresh and keeping it so ;
whereas fish-meal will keep for many months.   Beyond all,
it is a mistake to feed stock fish on horse-flesh, for diseased
ovaries will surely result in the case of the females.   However, it may become necessary to give the matured spawners
and milters something in addition to the supply of natural
food and fish-meal, and if this is so, then fresh sea-fish run
through the chopper is to be preferred to any other form of
food ; but care should be taken that no fatty fish, such as
herring, be given.   Clams will be found most useful to give
the eggs a nice, rich pink colour, and at any time, and under
any circumstances, they form most valuable food for mature
fish ; the one objection to them being the matter of expense.

Before concluding my remarks on rearing fry, I would
draw attention to a contrivance of which I give an illustration, and which Herr S. Jaffe, who first introduced it to notice,
describes as follows :—

"I raise my rainbows from the yolk sac stage in floating
boxes, and I think that, with proper management, these
would be a material help in raising them in the open stream
anywhere up to, say, May, and turning them out largely and
cheaply.   The boxes are the length of a sheet of perforated
zinc (two yards) ; the bottom of 1½in. boards tightly nailed
up with rat-proof cover.   The zinc is perforated, No. 9, and
the box is anchored to a chain and pole in the stream.
In the illustration the perforated zinc is marked A ; B is the
framed lid, which protects the fish from any outside enemies ;
and C is a strong ledge that, in addition to strengthening the contrivance, forms a platform on which

the attendant may stand when feeding the fish. Twenty
thousand fry are stocked to each box, and they are
fed three times a day much as other trout fry are. I have
had twelve of these boxes for five years in a mill-stream,
exposed to very strong freshets, and I find that each box
turns out from 12,000 to 17,000 two-inch healthy rainbows
in May. I have kept fry in them for experiment sake till
October (thinning them down to 5,000); but, although the
fish kept healthy, and fed well, they turned out in the end

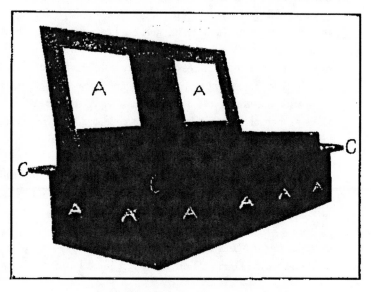

A FLOATING REARING BOX OUT OF WATER.

undersized and uneven. I have hatched fully-eyed ova in
these floating boxes, hanging up perforated trays two inches
from the bottom, and have done quite well with them. The
boxes require a fairly strong stream, the stronger the better,
and keep the fry wonderfully compact for feeding, and protected during their babyhood. I should think where proper
attendance cannot be secured the boxes ought not to be
tried. Where the boxes can be worked by a skilled attendant on some side-stream to the main body of water, they
will certainly prove a cheap and effective way of planting
rainbows, the fully-eyed eggs only having to be bought and
hatched on the spot."

CHAPTER XV.

A FEW CONCLUDING REMARKS.

I am rapidly reaching the end of my task; there remains only this chapter to complete my present contribution to the literature of fish-culture. In glancing over the pages already written, I am more than ever impressed with the vast possibilities of the subject, for so much remains unsaid; yet to have written more would have destroyed, to a great extent, the principal object I had in writing at all, and which is clearly laid down in the first chapter. In these few concluding remarks, therefore, I propose to follow the same path of practical utility which I have all through endeavoured to keep to.

The fact that " Fish Farming for Pleasure and Profit" has appeared in serial form in the columns of a widely-read sporting paper has naturally brought about some criticism as the work has progressed, and for upwards of nine months I have alternately deplored condemnation or rejoiced at praise as one or the other has been showered upon me. I am content knowing that praise predominates. I am delighted that my explanation of approved methods of fish-culture—successfully carried out in various parts of the kingdom—has clearly demonstrated the possibility of that which—in some cases—has hitherto been considered impossible, or, at least, beset by great difficulties. I am not so foolish as to think that my little book will entirely eradicate the prejudice against the pursuit of fish-culture; but I do hope—and believe—it may help those who are anxious to help themselves—and if I have succeeded in showing a way through a much tangled country I am content to accept the verdict of those who follow the road I have endeavoured to make clear.

The main object of the operations and apparatus recommended is to absolutely secure the safety of, and provide an ample supply of, food for the greatest possible number of fish until they arrive at a stage when they may be utilised for sporting or market purposes. Herein lies the secret of successful fish-farming. Trout eggs are so easily and cheaply obtained that an enormous number may be placed on redds or in hatcheries at a cost of a few pounds only. But success lies not in the direction of merely planting eggs; it is to be met with where, from the time of incubation until the fish arrive at maturity, they are absolutely secure, and their surroundings of a character to encourage healthy growth. I may well be excused for repeating here that placing some thousands of fry or yearlings in a water not properly prepared for their reception does not mean the successful stocking of that water. Let the security of your stock of fish and an ample food supply be your constant care and attention, and you will have no cause to regret embarking on fish-culture operations.

Should you have the slightest doubt about the suitability of a water when contemplating the formation or extension of a fishery, test it first on a small scale by the introduction of a few trout before committing yourself to operations of more importance. This advice applies specially to taking over an old fishery. There may exist some reason for its abandonment in the past, which utterly precludes successful operations to-day. On the other hand, such reasons may have existed in the past and do not obtain in the present.

Make firm friends of your neighbours, especially if they have any rights of access to your water supply from above.

Let your man in charge live close by the fishery. It may quite easily happen that a little timely attention will be the means of avoiding disaster.

With ordinary care, your stock of fish should be easily protected from their numerous enemies. In another place I

refer to those enemies that live actually amidst the natural
food of the fish; therefore, I need only caution you here
against the depredations of otters, herons, rats, mice, moles,
snakes, kingfishers, rabbits, cats—and men! With the exception of the latter, all of these should be destroyed or driven
away, or in some way prevented from interfering with your
stock of fish as fast as they put in an appearance. Once let
them get the upper hand, and good-bye to your fish-culture
operations! Trapping is the best method of getting rid of
these pests, and it is much to be preferred to shooting them,
as, after a time, they get too artful to permit of a successful
raid with a shot-gun, and yet continue to find opportunity
for their work of destruction. You cannot do better than
apply to Hy. Lane, of Eagle Works, Wednesfield, Staffs, for
traps of all sorts, and also ask him to send you one of his
pamphlets on " Traps and Trapping."

Some people prefer netting the pests—or, rather, those
that can be netted. A capital net for kingfishers is a
very fine " drop net," made from silk. It is hung from
bough to bough across the water. The birds flying down the
brook or river touch the net, which meshes them and drops
with them. Netting kingfishers has the advantage of not
always destroying them. When uninjured they may be released, and, after meshing themselves in a drop net for a
few times, will keep clear of the fishery. I need hardly remind my readers that in some parts it is illegal to kill kingfishers at certain times of the year, but I strongly advise some
precaution being taken, at all times, against their depredations, for they are most destructive to trout fry, and will
sit and fish from a point of vantage all the day through, off
and on—mostly on! Rats may be netted by means of
" bolt " nets, and where rabbits abound they can quickly be
thinned out by means of long nets pegged out across their
runs, while the rabbits are out feeding; then " flush " them
with a good dog. Good people to apply to for all sorts of
nets, including draw nets for getting the fish from rearing
ponds, etc., are Henry A. Chorlton, of 308 Derby-street,

Bolton, and Aquila Hancock, of Deritend Bridge, Birmingham.

Under any circumstances, your dams and banks must be kept free from the inroad of the furred enemies to fish-life, and the fish themselves from the attentions of their feathered foes. And do not forget that mice are very destructive to fish eggs. A well-trained dog is a useful friend at any fishery.

In conclusion, I would tender the old advice "If at first you don't succeed, try again"; and, with the exercise of some common-sense on your part, you will soon be able to farm fish for profit, and will assuredly derive pleasure from the pursuit of fish-culture.

DOG BREAKING.

BY

"WILDFOWLER."

A Practical Treatise on the
Training and Management of
Shooting Dogs.

(PROFUSELY ILLUSTRATED.)

WITH A CHAPTER ON

- The Field Trial Winners of the -
Present Day.

BY

FRED. GRESHAM.

Bound in Cloth, price 2/-, Post Free, 2/3.

PUBLISHED BY

The Burlington Publishing Co.

(Limited ,

72 to 76 TEMPLE CHAMBERS, BOUVERIE ST.,

LONDON, E.C.

LONDON :

PRINTED BY THE BURLINGTON PUBLISHING CO., LIMITED
72-76 TEMPLE-CHAMBERS, BOUVERIE-STREET, E.C.